Measure Your Meeting Mastery

An easy quiz to check the health of your meetings. Have fun!

1) How would you describe the culture that governs your meetings?

a) Uncivilized anarchy (war at its worst)

b) The Mad Hatter's Tea Party (crazy chaos)

c) Supportive problem solving (disciplined teamwork)

2) What happens to the ideas in your meetings?

a) If we had to think of ideas, it would be work

b) We forget them

c) A scribe writes them on a chart pad

3) Are results obtained in your meetings?

a) We eat all the donuts

b) Sometimes

c) Yes!

4) Do your meetings have an agenda?

a) A what?

b) I saw one once

c) Yes!

ii

5) Who attends your meetings?

a) Everyone I know plus assorted strangers

b) Too many

c) Only those who can contribute

6) How long are your meetings?

a) I'll let you know when this one ends

b) All day

c) An hour or less

7) During a meeting do you:

a) Break a foam cup into bits

b) Prepare for the next meeting

c) Focus on the topic

8) When do you prepare for a meeting?

a) During the meeting

b) On the way to the meeting

c) Before the meeting

9) While someone is speaking, do you:

a) Wonder about the strength of plastic foams

b) Plan a reply

c) Listen empathically

10) What structured activities do you you use in your meetings?

a) We sit on chairs

b) Everyone leaves at the same time

c) The process tools described in this book

Answers

Score the following points: subtract 5 points for every (a), give yourself 1 point for every (b), and award yourself 5 points for every (c). If your total is:

Negative

You need this book now. Read it in the store.

Between zero and 10

Buy this book and read it before your next meeting.

Between 10 and 46

Good going! You use many techniques that help you control your time in meetings. Now, learn how to master the rest by reading those sections that you need.

A perfect score of 50

Congratulations. You undoubtedly appreciate the value of effective meetings and must know hundreds of people who could benefit from this book. Buy a dozen copies (just for starters); then call the publisher at (714) 528-1300 to ask about bulk discounts. Your associates will be glad you did.

Plese turn the page to gain hundreds of ideas on how to hold effective meetings.

Meetings in an Hour or Less...

Maryellen,
Best of success as you
realize your dreams.
Steve Kaye
2/1/96

by Steve Kaye

Published by:
Personal Quality
P.O. Box 208
Placentia, CA 92670

(714) 528-1300

Cover by Helen Butler

ISBN:
1-884110-51-7

For Cathy

Contents

Introduction

Why meetings fail

Most executives feel they spend too much time in meetings. They resent this, too, because they know the success of their business depends upon their leadership, not their endurance. They know that planning, communicating, and learning are essential leadership activities. And yet, meetings get in the way.

Hundreds of people tell me that their meetings fail for the following reasons.

▶ It's business as usual. Many people are caught in a whirlwind schedule of marathon meetings. They go to meetings because everyone goes to meetings. *That's business*, they shrug. *We have to go.*

▶ People are fooled by short cuts. Preparing an agenda, for example, takes time. So, a chairperson takes a short cut by calling a meeting without an agenda, assuming the participants will arrive with a consistent vision of the issues supported by a common plan. We know how easily this results in long unproductive meetings.

▶ People lack modern tools. Many meetings are conducted with the old-fashioned communication process known as chit chat. This serves well at informal gatherings where the purpose is to communicate without making progress on anything in particular. Occasionally it can prove useful in a meeting, such as when people need to relax.

This book shows you how to avoid wasteful meetings. It contains easy, practical techniques that can help you gather information, reach consensus, and control problems. I have successfully applied these techniques to different types of meetings—meetings with executives, workers, and citizens—over the past years, and the results have always been the same: people accomplished more in less time.

Section 1
The Idea Harvest

Step 1:
Collect Ideas

The following process tools gather the information, knowledge, and wisdom held by your group. They provide maps that guide people through jungles of possibilities and up mountains of creativity to reach new levels of innovation. They bind people into intellectual teams that accomplish more than any group of individuals.

Use these tools to manage the dialogue in your meetings. They will help you accomplish more in less time.

Chapter 1

Process Tools
How to Make Them Work

What they are

Process tools are structured activities that lead to results. They use structures such as specific steps, limited time, or uniform participation. In meetings, such tools help people achieve results through focused communication, thinking, and analysis.

Save the unstructured activities for parties, holidays, and vacations.

Applications

Use these process tools any time you want a group to:

▶ Collect information

▶ Exchange information

▶ Develop solutions

▶ Find innovations

▶ Analyze situations

▶ Reach consensus

They also help a group work efficiently and effectively as a team by promoting equitable participation.

People have a remarkable ability to misunderstand vague requests.

How they work

These general steps apply to all the process tools.

1) Present every issue as a question. This focuses the participants' attention on the same approach to the issue.

For example, if you ask, *How can we reduce our budget by 10%?* everyone will focus on ways to reduce the budget by 10%.

If, however, you say *Let's talk about the budget,* different participants might think you want to talk about:

Ways to reduce the budget.

Ways to increase the budget.

Ways to allocate more funds to their department.

The inequity of arcane bureaucratic constraints.

A celebrity named Brigitte.

Questions are powerful because they define an issue. Thus, when preparing an agenda, plan specific questions that lead to the results you want.

2) Acknowledge everyone's contributions by writing the ideas on chart paper.

This is an essential step because it:

▶ Focuses attention on the issue

▶ Prevents duplicate contributions

▶ Captures contributions for minutes

▶ Makes people feel important

▶ Acknowledges the first person to think of an idea

▶ Results in a smoother, more productive meeting

3) Summarize results. After each activity tell the participants what they have finished. This serves to announce transitions, report accomplishments, and confirm decisions. For example, you could say:

That completes our brainstorm. (a transition)

We just collected 35 ideas to increase sales. (an accomplishment)

So, you prefer to advertise with a direct mail campaign? (a decision)

What they do

These process tools use the combined wisdom, experience, and needs of a group to obtain results. Indirectly, these tools also promote teamwork, build self-esteem, and create success.

What to expect

Your meetings will complete more work in less time. The participants will feel they have a role in the business and will enjoy your meetings.

Tip #1

Always evaluate whether the process tool is contributing to the result or hindering it. These tools are the means to the end, not the end itself. Thus, you should be flexible and willing to discard, alter, or invent tools as appropriate.

Important point

Tip #2

Let the participants decide (or at least agree upon) which tools you use. This promotes cooperation and represents true facilitation.

Tip #3

In general, if you are the chairperson or the facilitator avoid side comments, jokes, and unrelated issues. Although entertaining, they distract everyone from the issue and make the meeting less productive.

Tip #4

Use questions to guide the dialogue. Questions identify directions, focus attention, and confirm decisions.

Variation on the process

Although these tools are presented as group activities, you can also use them as an individual. They offer the advantages of focusing your attention, involving your senses, and recording your thoughts.

Key Ideas

▶ Present issues as questions to focus thinking toward a specific result.

▶ Acknowledge all ideas offered during the process. This rewards participants and maintains focus on the issue.

Chapter 2

Brainstorms

Mental Popcorn

What it is

Participants accumulate a large quantity of ideas hoping that at least one of them proves useful. Ideally, the participants are curious, open, and playful. Their pace, however, is fast, dynamic, and intense. A brainstorm can feel like a wild romp through the Garden of Nonsense. And it can produce amazing innovations.

The negative aspects of brainstorms are: 1) they collect a large quantity of low-quality ideas, 2) individual recognition is lost, and 3) some groups use them for every issue (when there may be more effective process tools).

Applications

Use this process when you need new ideas or an innovation.

How it works

1) The facilitator starts the process by asking a question, such as:

Ask people to bring their brains, too.

How can we get people to pay their bills on time?

What is a new way to fasten metal to wood?

What can we name our lawn mower?

2) The participants offer ideas and the scribe (see the Glossary for definitions) writes all of them on chart paper.

3) Throughout the idea collection the facilitator creates and maintains a high energy level. The facilitator should move about, clap, laugh, shout praise, call on people, and ask questions. Questions are an essential element in a brainstorm because they spark creative thinking.

Essential rules

A brainstorm depends upon childlike spontaneity to succeed. Thus, the participants must:

▶ Suspend judgment

▶ Ignore *How?*

▶ Avoid rationalizations

▶ Build on other ideas

▶ Go for quantity

▶ Be spontaneous

▶ Support each other

▶ Have fun

Remember, a brainstorm is a chaotic, crazy sprint rather than a dignified stroll through ideas.

What it does

This process produces a large quantity of ideas, some of which may be novel and useful.

What to expect

Most of the initial ideas will be old news. Identifying these is an essential step in finding novel ideas.

Collecting known ideas may also prove useful if it has never been done before. This documents the status quo for the issue.

Skilled participants talk fast, laugh easily, and congratulate each other. They make the process chaotic and crazy. You should encourage this because you want a mad cauldron of creativity that boils over, flooding the charts with novel ideas.

Tip #1

The facilitator should create a safe, relaxed environment by telling jokes, laughing, or playing. Bring toys (such as balloons, balls, or stuffed animals), blow bubbles, and act playful. This shows everyone that it is safe to consider unconventional ideas.

One important caution: jokes, play, and fun must be in good taste. Avoid all jokes that offend, threaten, or hurt others. There is, of course, only one safe target for humor, and that is ourselves.

It is wise to test humor before playing it before an audience. If at least three associates from different backgrounds agree that a gag is funny, then you can

A funny thing happened to me on the way to the meeting.

expect it is probably safe. If one person shows even a mildly negative reaction, then you need to revise or eliminate the gag.

Important point

Tip #2

Avoid criticism. The fastest way to ruin a brainstorm is to have someone say, *That's a dumb idea,* or *That won't work,* or *How in the world would you do that?* It's like having an angry voice yell at happy children. Their creativity stops.

Tip #3

Avoid analysis while collecting ideas. For example, suppose someone said, *We should eliminate first-line approval on purchase orders because the manager and the vice-president always approve orders before they go to the president for approval. So, this would eliminate a step and save time, if the supervisors don't mind. Of course, I know my supervisor likes to approve purchase orders, but we need to simplify the process and maybe we could just ....* Can you feel yourself becoming bored with this?

If someone begins analyzing an idea, interrupt by saying, *Excuse me, I know that's important and we'll consider it later. Right now we need ideas.*

Tip #4

Offer concise ideas. Reread the example in Tip #3 and notice how a long rambling statement induces sleep. If you present ideas with volumes of supporting analysis, you will have the same effect in your meeting.

Brief, clear statements work best. For example, instead of the long, complicated statement in Tip #3, you might call out, *Eliminate first line approval!*

Tip #5
Avoid justifying ideas. This has the same impact as analysis: it quenches creativity.

Tip #6
Avoid judgment. All ideas during a brainstorm are *Fantastic!* There are no bad ideas. Amazing ideas will energize the participants to think of something else.

Tip #7
If you are a participant, jot down your own ideas while others talk. This captures your valuable ideas so you can contribute them when a pause occurs in the Idea Harvest.

Tip #8
If you are the facilitator, spark ideas by asking strange questions that cause people to view things in new ways, such as:

Seek out incredible possibilities.

What do feet like about shoes?

How could we sell our paper to a copy machine?

What could we add that would make this smaller?

What if it had no wheels?

What if it had wheels?

What if the wheels were inside?

How would the product want to be packaged so it arrived in good shape?

What name would a child give this?

What would we want to happen if we lived inside the machine?

What would we hear if we had the same color eyes?

What would it be like to run along beside a light beam at the speed of light?

You may think some of these questions sound stupid. And that's the point. Absurd possibilities rattle people's thinking to shake free new ideas. They provide the creative grit that leads to pearls of genius. Part of Einstein's success came from asking unthinkable questions.

Before conducting a brainstorm, prepare a list of questions that spark creative thinking or suggest valuable possibilities. Then use these questions if the flow of ideas slows. You will think of more questions during the brainstorm.

Of course, remember that you are using questions to spark thinking, not control it. The group may run off in a different direction than you expected, and in a brainstorm that's okay.

Tip #9

Everyone should offer encouragement to other members of the group. If you are a participant, say:

Wow!

That's great!

Fantastic!

People want to feel that their ideas contribute to the process. This includes ideas that they know are dumb. So, it is especially important that the facilitator support the team with generous encouragement.

Tip #10

The facilitator can push for more ideas by saying:

I want two more ideas.

Pat, what do you think?

Give me an idea, Chris!

Ask for what you need to succeed.

Asking for one or two more ideas stretches the group's thinking. Usually, the group finds more.

Tip #11

The facilitator should ask quiet participants for ideas. This pulls the person into the brainstorm and shows the group that everyone is expected to contribute. If the person remains silent, say something like, *That's okay,* or *Keep thinking.* Then collect an idea from someone else.

Tip #12

Plan brainstorms that last a short time. Often 5 to 10 minutes is enough. Of course, there can be exceptions. Some issues may benefit from longer sessions. When writing a novel I once spent half an hour writing a list of 80 names before finding the name that suited a character.

Tip #13

Have everyone stand during the brainstorm. People are more creative when they are moving. (A truly dynamic brainstorm session will bring the participants to their feet.)

Variations on the Process

Extravaganza

Give your brainstorms extra prestige by calling them The World Sillies, The Smiley Cup Championship, or The Super Brains Bowl.

Team Spirit

Make team tee shirts with a creative logo and wear them during brainstorms.

Make It a Game

Divide the participants into groups (e.g., four or five per group) and award a prize to the group with the most ideas at the end of 4 or 5 minutes.

Add excitement by conducting a relay race, where each team member serves as the scribe/facilitator for a minute. Run enough laps so every team member receives at least one turn as the scribe/facilitator. If there are different numbers of people on the teams, some member will take two turns. Signal when it's time to change facilitators with a whistle or horn.

Possible prizes include cookies, free meals in the cafeteria, preferred parking spaces, tickets worth an hour of vacation, gift certificates, or a 3-month holiday at a 5-star resort.

When I conduct relay race brainstorms during my workshops on Effective Meetings, the enthusiasm is electric. Everyone stands. People cheer. And the combined list of ideas exceeds what a single group would have collected in twice the time.

Race to the Finish
Challenge the teams to be the first to collect 100 different ideas. (Expect some argument over what constitutes uniquely different ideas.)

Divide and Prosper
Conduct the brainstorm in two brief sessions separated by a break or a meal. People often find new insights after a period of reflection.

Example application

A Shot in the Dark Pays Off
I was facilitating a brainstorm session to design a theme for a conference. The group wanted a special idea that would attract a large attendance. At first they seemed stuck. Everyone sat silently staring off into space. So in desperation, I called out, *Give me a noun.*

Ball, someone replied.

That seemed like a dead end, so I asked, *Where do you use a ball?*

For sports, someone said.

This felt more useful. *Name a sport,* I said.

Bounce new ideas off people's heads.

Soccer, someone said.

Ah ha! Here was a possibility. *How can this event be like a soccer match?* I asked.

Suddenly ideas began to crackle. Now the group was planning a soccer tournament. From this came ideas for activities, table decorations, promotional materials, and refreshments. Within ten minutes, they had designed a conference with a soccer theme that promised to be different, exciting, and fun.

Key Ideas

▶ Use brainstorms to find novel ideas.

▶ A brainstorm is a wild romp through varied possibilities. It is hoped that at least one of the many ideas proves useful.

▶ Brainstorms depend on a safe childlike environment to succeed. Suspend judgment, ignore how, avoid analysis, and just let the ideas flow.

Chapter 3

Balanced Dialogue

A Fair Share for All

What it is

Each participant receives an equal time to state views on an issue. By controlling the time for discussion, this process tool helps people prepare, focus, and prioritize their contributions. It also reduces low value contributions.

Applications

Use this process any time a group wants to discuss:

▶ Reports in staff meetings (a typical information exchange)

▶ Viewpoints on an issue

▶ Introductions at the beginning of a conference or large meeting

How it works

1) Give the participants a moment to prepare by saying:

Let's take a minute to organize our thoughts, okay?

This tool is a powerful time saver.

Then start the clock. At the end of a minute, say:

Okay, time's up.

Time.

Generally, a minute of preparation is sufficient.

2) Everyone speaks for an equal amount of time. Begin this step by asking:

Who wants to go first?

Either the facilitator or the scribe keeps time, starting the clock with the first word uttered. If you want to, you can count nonverbal sounds such as ah, um, and humphh. When the time expires, the facilitator signals by saying:

Next?

It is important that the participants enforce this tool by stopping the speaker when the time expires, even if the speaker is in the middle of a word. Without enforcement, the process reverts to an inefficient freeform discussion.

Generally, social pressure will stop a speaker because most people want to cooperate. If someone attempts to keep talking, you can invite everyone to applaud at the end of each person's time.

One to two minutes suffices for most issues, and sometimes half a minute is enough. If you are the facilitator ask the group to select (or agree upon) the time. I prefer slightly too little versus too much time because this challenges people to focus their ideas.

What it does

This process manages an equitable exchange of ideas within a set time limit.

What to expect

Everyone will speak faster, with more intensity. They will prioritize their ideas and present them concisely. You will hear bullet-point presentations. Most people will finish within the time limit.

This made me think before I spoke.

Some people will want to speak first because they want the first word. Others will wait until last because they want the rebuttal.

Someone will challenge the time limit the first time you use this technique. After all, that person has spoken at length in the past. When you stop this person, expect to receive a scowl that could crush rock. Ignore it and move on. Next time that person will speak more concisely.

Someone may want to bank unused time for the next balanced dialogue. Instead, welcome unused time as contributions toward a shorter meeting. If the participants want more control over their speaking times, you can use the Pay Per Viewpoint variation described below.

Someone may want to donate time to another participant. This defeats the intent of the process and should

A stopwatch is essential equipment for meetings.

be discouraged. The benefit of a balanced dialogue is that everyone receives an equal time to speak.

Tip #1

Bring a stopwatch to meetings. Then you will be able to time presentations in a balanced dialogue.

Tip #2

Use this technique to control discussions on controversial issues. It allows each person to speak while preventing any one person from dominating.

If a discussion becomes a shouting match, you can (sometimes) restore order by calling for a balanced dialogue.

Tip #3

Insist that the speaker receive exclusive air time. Other participants should keep their questions, comments, and interruptions for other parts of the meeting.

Tip #4

Always ask the participants to select the amount of time they will have to prepare and to speak. You can direct their choices by asking:

I suggest we take a minute to prepare our thoughts. Is that enough time?

Is it okay if each person speaks for two minutes on this?

This obtains their agreement that enough time was provided to prepare and express their views.

Tip #5

When appropriate, save time by asking the participants to prepare their comments before the meeting.
This works best when the topic is fully known before
the meeting, such as reports in a staff meeting or
introductions before a large meeting.

Tip #6

A committee chair can use a balanced dialogue to
introduce the members of a committee in their first
meeting. In this case, each person could receive 5 to 10
minutes to describe their background, expectations,
and concerns.

Convening a committee with introductions produces
the following important benefits:

▶ You learn about resources. This identifies who can
help as well as who will need help with projects.

▶ You learn who supports or opposes the issues. This
helps plan private discussions that may be necessary to facilitate completing the project.

▶ You learn the member's preferred behavior and
communication styles. This helps you guide future
meetings.

▶ You eliminate hidden agendas. Most committee
members will use this time to make philosophical
statements, describe expectations, and state personal
goals. By providing time for these comments at the
beginning of the committee process you avoid
having the participants work them into subsequent
meetings, when it could reduce productivity.

Everyone has a
hidden agenda.

Tip #7

Use a balanced dialogue any time during a meeting when the participants want to discuss an issue.

Variations on the Process

Pay Per Viewpoint

The participants receive equal numbers of tokens that they use to buy speaking time. Participants can then allocate their speaking time according to the number and value of their tokens.

This trades some complexity for more flexibility.

For example, if you gave each person six 30-second tokens they could spend:

▶ All six tokens on one 3-minute statement

▶ Each token separately, making six 30-second statements

▶ The tokens in groups, such as three tokens, two tokens, and one token

This approach has the advantage of providing flexibility while limiting each person's total talking time.

Treat the tokens the same as time intervals in a standard balanced dialogue. The participants must stop when their time is up and unused time contributes to a shorter meeting. If you want more flexibility, you can use more tokens with shorter time spans. Of course, this increases the complexity of the process.

Also, I recommend that you prohibit trading, selling, or donating tokens.

Mixed Format

Often people want to comment or ask questions after someone speaks. Accommodate this by setting a time period after each presentation for general discussion.

It is essential that you keep this discussion period short (e.g., 2 to 5 minutes) and enforce the time limits. Otherwise, this process quickly degenerates into an unstructured discussion.

When you introduce this process, encourage the participants to keep their questions, comments, and answers as brief as possible.

Example application

Controversy Contained

A major corporation convened a committee to design a software system for their engineers. The system was supposed to provide software and performance data that would help engineers design equipment, plan maintenance, and monitor operations.

Each member of the committee represented a different sector of the business—research, technical service, foreign operations, and four domestic regions.

Discussions frequently became stuck when some committee members tried to convince other members that they should adopt features that supported local interests.

This was resolved by holding balanced dialogues. Now, each committee member had an equal chance to present views on an issue. As a result, controversy was contained and progress made.

The committee completed its work in record time and received praise for a job well done.'

Key Ideas

▶ In a balanced dialogue each person receives an equal (short) time to state views on an issue. By controlling the time for discussion, this process tool helps people prepare, focus, and prioritize their contributions. It also reduces low value contributions.

▶ Use a balanced dialogue any time the group wants to discuss an issue.

Chapter 4

Force Field Analysis

Explore Differences

What it is

This process gathers ideas for issues with opposing
sides. It is similar to the famous Ben Franklin analysis
(see Glossary) conducted with a group.

Applications

Use this process to analyze issues with two opposing
viewpoints. The results can support decisions, identify contingency plans, or uncover solutions.

Usually the two viewpoints are the pros versus the
cons. For example:

Why do customers buy versus *reject a product?*

Why should we do something versus *not do it?*

What would cause a project to succeed versus *fail?*

How does a policy motivate employees versus *discourage
them?*

How is this strategy an improvement versus *a liability?*

Why Move?	Why Stay?

How it works

1) The scribe writes the issue at the top of a chart paper, draws a large T, and then writes each viewpoint (such as Pro and Con or Why? and Why not?) above opposite sides of the T.

2) The participants offer ideas for the different viewpoints.

What it does

This process helps a group view an issue from both sides.

What to expect

Participants will offer ideas that describe both sides of an issue. Often, an idea for one view will cause someone to think of an opposing idea. For example:

It's a plus that working overtime builds character.

Oh yeah? It's a negative that working overtime builds characters.

Sometimes ideas will appear on both sides of the line as equivalent statements or as inverse statements, such as:

Issue: Should we declare Friday a casual day?

▶ Pro: *Casual clothes feel comfortable* (original statement)

▶ Con: *People feel relaxed in casual clothes* (equivalent statement)

▶ Con: *People feel less businesslike in casual clothes*
(inverse statement)

Tip #1

Explore if ideas submitted for one view lead to an
idea for the opposing view. This helps find all the
possibilities for the issue.

Tip #2

Use a separate chart for each viewpoint to provide
more writing space for ideas.

Tip #3

Encourage the participants to offer ideas for both
viewpoints, rather than collecting one view followed
by the other.

Tip #4

Expect to collect unpopular and controversial ideas.
When these arrive, remain neutral and thank the
participants for offering them. If you act disappointed
or attempt to argue with the participants, you will
discourage further candid contributions.

The goal is to find all the ideas.

Tip #5

When selecting ways to cause change, it is often more
effective to remove obstacles than to apply more
force. That is, people will cooperate more readily to
gain a carrot than to avoid a stick.

Variations on the Process

Multidimensional Analysis

Explore complex force fields with more than two dimensions. For example, the issue *In which region should we build a new warehouse?* could have 6 dimensions.

▶ For the West Coast

▶ Against the West Coast

▶ For the Midwest

▶ Against the Midwest

▶ For the East Coast

▶ Against the East Coast

When using this approach, you will need a large writing area to capture ideas for all the dimensions. Make one by covering a wall with chart paper or by using many chart pads.

Note: Use an extra sheet of paper as backing to prevent bleed-through by the marking pens.

A multidimensional force field analysis has the advantage of considering the entire picture. Of course, you can also work on complex issues by dividing them into two dimensional issues.

Consider Consequences

Use a force field analysis to identify possible consequences of decisions to help with planning. For example:

If we were to carry out this policy, how might employees accept it versus oppose it?

If we were to make this product, why would customers want it versus reject it?

If we made this decision, what desirable versus undesirable results might occur?

What if an accident occurred? How would people support us versus oppose us?

What if a competitor produced a similar product? Why would people buy from us versus from them?

Example application

An automobile manufacturer was about to introduce a new model car. Since this represented a venture into a different market, the company wondered how their customers might react.

The managers responsible for the dealerships conducted a force field analysis. They considered, *Why customers would want to buy the car* versus *Why customers would reject it.*

The results of their analysis helped them prepare answers to potential customer concerns and also to identify notable benefits. Thus, they were able to

advise their dealers on the most effective way to promote the new car.

Key Ideas

▶ Use a force field analysis to collect opposing viewpoints on an issue.

▶ To conduct a force field analysis, draw a T on a sheet of paper, write the viewpoints above opposite sides of the T, and collect ideas for these viewpoints.

▶ This process also uncovers possible consequences, which assists with contingency planning.

Chapter 5

Cause and Effect

Diagrams That Show Why

What it is

This process tool helps people identify causes that contribute to an effect. It does this by providing a structure for discovering and collecting those causes.

Dr. Kaoru Ishikawa of the University of Tokyo introduced this tool during the summer of 1943 when he showed engineers at Kawasaki Steel Works how to sort out and relate the factors affecting a process.

Applications

Use this tool to understand why something happens. Usually, people conduct a cause and effect analysis to identify needed improvements by asking:

What causes the Centerville plant to produce 5% more waste?

What causes higher employee turnover in the corporate office?

What causes poor sales in Region 3?

Sometimes the causes pile up.

A cause and effect analysis can also identify the causes for successes, such as:

Why does the Centerville plant have a better safety record?

What would characterize a successful marketing program?

What are the design features of a successful product?

How it works

1) Select categories of causes related to the issue. The most common categories are People, Procedures, Equipment, and Materials.

Depending upon the issue, other categories may be more appropriate. Possibilities include attitudes, competition, culture, customers, environment, labor, leadership, location, management, measurement, policies, research staff, regulations, sales staff, strategies, or technology.

Most cause and effect diagrams have four branches and look like:

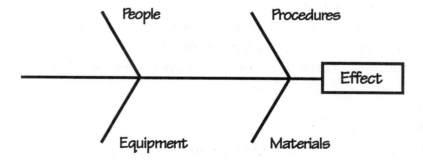

Of course, you can use any number of branches that describes the issue as long as each branch represents an independent category. Avoid similar categories, such as People and Labor, because these lead to duplicate listings and confusion working with the results.

2) Collect ideas from the participants on the causes related to each category. The result will look like a large fish bone diagram (see page 35).

Such a diagram requires a large writing area. Prepare one by covering a large, empty wall with chart paper. Be sure to use an extra sheet of paper as a backing to prevent bleed-through by the marking pens.

You can also use a separate chart pad for each category. For Example:

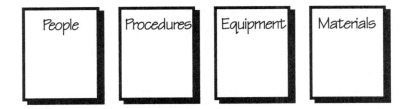

What it does
This process organizes the causes of an issue into appropriate categories. By forming branches, you will identify sequences of related causes, which show the complexity of the issue.

What to expect
Most of the ideas will be common knowledge. A few may be surprises. The overall result, however, will show an organized description of why the effect occurs.

You may be surprised by what you collect.

Tip #1

When someone announces an idea without a category, ask the group, *Where should I put this?* Then wait for them to tell you.

Tip #2

If the group has different opinions on where to place an idea, let them discuss it briefly. If they seem undecided, suggest putting the idea in more than one place. The participants will be able to refine and prioritize their ideas in subsequent steps.

Tip #3

Draw the basic fish bone diagram with the category titles before the meeting. This saves time starting the process.

Tip #4

If the diagram becomes large with extensive branching, explore if complexity, red tape, and bureaucracy contribute to the effect.

Tip #5

Use at least two scribes. This is especially important for very large diagrams. (See Tip #6)

Tip #6

Ask members of the group to serve as scribes. This way, you can have a scribe for each category.

Then rotate the role of scribe with a new set of volunteers, so that the original scribes can contribute ideas. I like to change scribes two to three times during this process. It involves everyone and makes the process dynamic.

Tip #7

Ask the participants to contribute ideas for specific categories. This is especially effective for categories that receive fewer ideas. For example, ask:

Does anyone have an idea for equipment?

How about materials?

I need some ideas for procedures.

Variations on the Process

The Other Side of the Mirror

Sometimes it can be more effective (and fun) to approach an issue from its negative side. For example, instead of identifying the attributes (causes) of an effective meeting, you could ask the group to design an absolutely disappointing, disgusting, dreadful meeting.

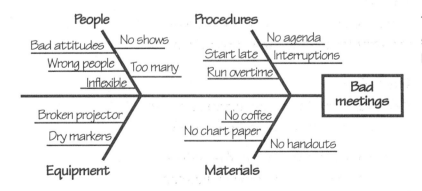

This is an example of a simple Cause and Effect Diagram.

This approach makes it easier for the participants to contribute controversial ideas. Instead of complaining, the participants create a caricature of the situation. It's fun and feels safe.

After collecting ideas in this process, the next step is to plan for the opposite. If, for example, you designed a disastrous meeting, the next step would be to plan ways to prevent the causes from happening.

Property and Product Diagram
Use a cause and effect diagram to design things. Select categories for properties, draw the structure, and collect the properties that lead to a successful product. For example, if you were designing a bicycle, the categories might be frame, wheels, brakes, drive system, and seat.

Key Ideas
▶ Cause and effect diagrams identify reasons.

▶ To conduct a cause and effect analysis, draw a branch diagram, label the branches with appropriate categories (such as People, Procedures, Equipment, and Materials), and collect causes related to each category.

▶ Use cause and effect diagrams to improve situations or design products.

Chapter 6

NGT

Nominal Group Technique

What it is
This tool provides a formal structure for gathering, discussing, and voting on options.

Application
Use this process to find and select solutions.

For example, after identifying the major cause of a problem (with the cause and effect diagram), you could conduct a nominal group technique to find the best way to deal with that cause.

How it works
1) Present the issue as a question. For example:

How can we reduce spending to finish the year within budget?

What marketing strategies will effectively promote this product?

This is a real power tool.

What changes must we make to comply with the new regulations?

2) Ask the participants to make a list of ideas. If this step is done during the meeting, set a time limit of one to two minutes.

Complex issues that require research should be announced in the agenda so the participants can plan ideas before the meeting.

3) Collect ideas using a round robin. This gives everyone an opportunity to contribute.

When participants run out of ideas, they should pass. If they think of new ideas, they can offer them on their next turn.

Continue this step until all ideas have been collected.

Important point

Avoid rationalizations, explanations, and justifications during this part of the process. Such statements slow the process and inhibit participation. The participants will be able to analyze the ideas in the next step.

4) Refine ideas. The group will recognize that some of the ideas convey identical thoughts. Examine these ideas for opportunities to combine those that are similar and to eliminate duplicates.

5) Discuss ideas. Ideally, use a balanced dialogue (Chapter 3) to present rationalizations, explanations, implications, and justifications for the ideas.

If you use a standard discussion, see Chapter 9 for tips on how to maximize its outcome.

6) Vote. You can use dot voting, show of hands, or ballots (see Section 2 for the tools). This brings closure to the process by selecting the preferred options.

What it does
This process helps a group find the best option for an issue.

What to expect
This is often a more serious process than a brainstorm. The participants make lists of ideas, offer them, analyze them, and select the ones they like the most.

The structure of this process creates an atmosphere of fairness in resolving an issue or in selecting a solution. It also drives the group toward obtaining a result.

Tip #1
If you are a participant, jot down new ideas as you think of them, so you can contribute them when it is your turn.

Tip #2
Write down questions, arguments, and rebuttals as you think of them during the Information Harvest. This will ensure that you retain these ideas for the discussion part of the process.

Tip #3
Ask the participants to prepare a list of ideas in the agenda. Then distribute the agenda well before the

meeting. This is especially helpful for complex issues that require research.

Tip #4

If the issue is sufficiently complex, you should collect and distribute copies of everyone's proposed solutions before the meeting. This enables the participants to analyze the solutions before they evaluate them.

Variation on the process

Ghost Writers in the Sky

Sometimes an issue is so controversial that people are reluctant to propose solutions. Here is an approach that masks the origin of ideas.

The participants write their ideas on index cards. Then the cards are collected, shuffled, and distributed face down to the participants. The participants look at their cards but should not show them to others. They may want to organize them in order of priority.

I can think of a better idea than this.

Ideas are collected in a round robin. Each participant picks up a card, looks at it and decides:

▶ To read the idea on the card

▶ To offer a different idea (it could be a new idea or a different idea)

▶ To ignore the idea on the card and pass

Then the participant places the card on the bottom of the stack, where it can launch another new (or different) idea. Thus, it is unimportant if a participant receives a different number of cards (ideas) than submitted.

Collect ideas until all the participants pass. Then continue with steps 4 through 6 of the standard nominal group technique.

Example application

Process Improvement
Six team leaders from a plant that manufactured office supplies wanted to improve operating efficiency. After selecting the most important manufacturing procedure, they applied the nominal group technique to identify improvements.

After preparing their lists of ideas, the participants collected a dozen ideas in a round robin. They eliminated one idea because it duplicated another and combined two similar ideas. Then they discussed the ideas with a balanced dialogue, where each participant spoke for a minute. Most of the participants used their time to cite the merits of their favorite ideas. Then the group prioritized the ideas according to two parameters—potential impact and ease of application.

When they finished, they had identified actions that most easily brought the greatest improvements to their most important procedure. This part of the meeting lasted about 20 minutes, which shows it's possible to complete a great deal of work in a short time with structured process tools.

Key Ideas

▶ The nominal group technique helps a group gather, evaluate, and prioritize ideas.

▶ The steps for a nominal group technique are: 1) Participants collect ideas, 2) they contribute their ideas in a round robin, 3) they discuss the ideas, and 4) they select the best idea.

▶ The participants should be asked to prepare their ideas for complex issues before the meeting.

Chapter 7

Affinity Diagram

Structured Disorder

What it is
This is a creative thinking process that collects and organizes ideas.

Applications
Use an affinity diagram to define concepts, visions, or global plans. Since the participants contribute ideas with some anonymity, this process makes it easy to propose unpopular ideas.

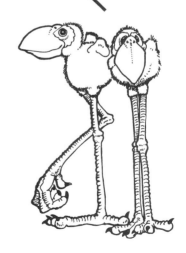

Ideas of a feather have an affinity for one another.

How it works
1) Write the issue on a paper, sign, or large Post-it™ Note. Then place this on a large, smooth surface, like the title above a work of art.

Ideal surfaces include painted walls, windows, or walls covered with 4 or 5 chart papers. Allow enough space for the participants to walk comfortably about as they post, read, and move ideas.

Idea

Idea

Idea

Idea

Idea

The ideas collect like autumn leaves.

2) Give each participant a pad of Post-it™ Notes and a marking pen. You can economize by splitting pads of Notes among participants, giving each person at least a fourth of a pad.

I recommend using pens that make a bold mark that can be read from at least 6 feet away.

3) The participants write ideas related to the issue on the Notes and silently post them on the surface. This is a dynamic process that works best when the participants stand.

4) If you are facilitating this process, encourage the participants to:

▶ Read the notes others have posted so they can build on their ideas.

▶ Add original ideas. Duplicate ideas, however, are okay because they will be combined in subsequent steps.

▶ Refrain from discussion, analysis, or explanation. The participants simply write ideas on Post-it™ Notes and place them on the wall.

Then assist with the process by asking leading questions. For example, if the issue was, *What is quality?* you could ask:

What does quality mean to our customers?

What do you expect of your staff?

What does your staff expect of you?

What does quality mean to our competition?

How would the leaders behave in a high quality company?

What would distinguish the employees in a high quality company?

What are you proud of?

Some of these questions ask for the same information from different viewpoints. This helps maximize everyone's contributions by touching different cues in their thinking.

Continue this step until the participants run out of ideas.

5) Announce the end of the Information Harvest. At this point, the wall should be covered with dozens (hundreds?) of randomly placed Post-it™ Notes.

6) The participants silently organize the ideas into groups that have an affinity for each other. During this part of the process any participant can move any idea or group of ideas. Stack duplicate ideas on top of each other.

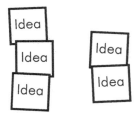

This is a highly iterative step. Some ideas will move, move again, and move again.

When the rearrangement slows it is time for the next step.

7) The participants assign titles to the groups of ideas. They can do this by writing the title on a different color or different size Post-it™ Note, or by simply rotating the title note 45 degrees. It is possible (and okay) for an idea to become a title.

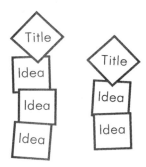

During this step the participants can continue to move and add ideas. They will want to do that, too, once they compare the ideas in a group with the title given that group.

The process ends when the participants stop moving ideas or naming groups of ideas. Ask everyone to step back, examine their work, and decide if they like the result.

What it does
This process collects and organizes ideas of conceptual issues.

What to expect
At the end of the idea posting step, the surface will look like a field covered with autumn leaves. Dozens (hundreds?) of randomly placed Post-it™ Notes will contain a wide range of ideas.

When finished, these notes will be organized into clusters of ideas that describe the issue.

An unpopular idea may appear almost mysteriously because no one noticed who posted it. The group may react with laughter or concern. If this happens, affirm that you welcome all ideas and encourage the group to continue.

During the rearrangement, some ideas may seem like orphans: no one adds them to a group. Point out these ideas and ask where they belong or if they represent a new category.

Tip #1
Make sure everyone stands for this process. People who sit contribute less, if anything.

Tip #2
Ask questions to help the participants explore all dimensions of the issue, challenge the affinity groupings, and check for consistency between titles and their ideas.

Tip #3
Approach less involved participants with one-on-one encouragements or thought-provoking questions.

Tip #4
When the Information Harvest slows, ask for one last round of thinking. For example, you could say:

I want two more ideas.

Okay, we have half a minute left.

When you announce the process is about to end people scramble to gather stray ideas.

Tip #5
When finished, use strips of cellophane tape to secure the notes to the chart paper or to transfer the notes to chart paper.

Variations on the process

Post and Shout!
The participants announce their ideas as they post them. This communicates ideas to the other participants and in turn, reduces duplicate ideas. This

makes the process more dynamic and noisy. It also removes the anonymity in the original process.

Secret Ballots

This variation increases anonymity at the expense of an extra step. Instead of posting their notes on a surface, the participants drop them in a box. Then someone (it could be the facilitator or a helper) removes the notes and places them on the surface. Notes should be posted as soon as possible to keep the process moving and to minimize duplicate ideas.

Define the Outline

Start an affinity diagram process with specified titles. Then the participants attach notes to the titles. Additional titles can be added if needed.

Everyone Helps Everyone

Each participant writes a title, issue, or question on a sign. The signs are posted on a wall and then the participants help each other by posting ideas on each other's signs.

This is an excellent networking exercise.

Awareness Expansion

The very exercise of working through an affinity diagram process can be educational for the participants. Thus, use an affinity diagram to raise the group's awareness of conceptual issues. For example, you could create an affinity diagram on integrity to define and emphasize the business ethics for your business.

Example application

A Mission in Record Time

An affinity diagram helped the six members of a work team write a mission statement for their team. They began by posting notes that described their responsibilities, values, skills, abilities, and work culture. Then they organized the notes into groups and assigned titles to the groups.

They proceeded with the following steps:

1) Form pairs. (For this group, there were three pairs.)

2) Each pair wrote a draft of a statement that captured the essence of the posted notes. (Working with a partner is more efficient and effective than working alone. It increases focus, combines knowledge, and challenges ideas.)

3) Each pair gave a brief presentation on their statement, explaining the logic behind it.

4) The draft statements were taped to the wall in the front of the conference room. This placed the drafts where everyone could study them.

5) The group used a discussion to combine the best from each statement into a single statement.

This entire process produced a mission statement in less than an hour.

In contrast, some organizations have spent hundreds of hours discussing a mission statement.

Key Ideas

▶ An affinity diagram uses Post-it™ Notes to collect ideas and organize them into a coherent statement.

▶ The participants write ideas on Post-it™ Notes, place the Notes on a large surface, organize the notes into groups, and select titles for the groups.

▶ Use affinity diagrams to describe concepts, visions, or global plans.

Chapter 8

Plus/Delta

Learning How to Improve

What it is

This process collects ideas on how to improve.

Applications

Use this process to design new systems, reengineer operations, or find opportunities for continuous improvement.

How it works

1) Begin by drawing a T on a chart and writing a **+** above the left side and a Δ above the right.

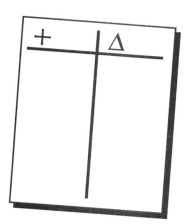

Then ask the group *What did you like?* while pointing to the plus and *What would you like to be different?* while pointing to the delta.

The words in the second question (**What would you like to be different?**) are very important because they direct the participants toward positive responses. We want suggestions for improvement instead of complaints about what failed.

Thus, avoid asking questions such as *What did you hate?* or *What went wrong?*

2) Collect the ideas and express appreciation for all of them. This will be challenging when you hear ideas that insult, attack, or misunderstand something you did.

Nevertheless, you must smile (or at least appear neutral) as you collect deltas.

Important point

If you react negatively to a delta, no matter how outrageous the delta may be, you will destroy the trust needed for this process to succeed. The participants will sense danger and stop contributing.

What it does
This process identifies things that expand excellence.

What to expect
Most participants begin by offering positive ideas. Even when the group feels disappointed, they start with good news.

While it feels gratifying to hear compliments, the most valuable ideas are the deltas. So, you want to encourage the participants to offer them.

Most deltas will be minor corrections you suspected before you started (yawn) and some deltas will burn your ears (ouch!). They will attack your best efforts, suggest impossible changes, and reveal complete misunderstandings. See Tip #1 (below).

Sometimes the same idea will appear as both a plus and a delta. For example, participants may comment on an air conditioned room by saying:

The room was comfortably cool. (a plus)

The room should be heated. (a delta)

Tip #1

Although you may strongly disagree with (and resent) some deltas, recognize that all the deltas are valuable. Realize that other people view the world from different perspectives than you do. Sometimes people notice things you thought were insignificant and sometimes people feel offended by things you feel proud of. In addition, sometimes suggestions for change sound offensive.

The deltas are the most important part of this process. They may uncover hidden opportunities as well as urgently needed changes. Collect them. Remain calm. Thank the participants. And consider how you can use them to improve.

The way you respond to difficult deltas tests your character.

Tip #2

Realize you can always ignore deltas. It's a fact that some deltas may be impossible. Yet, even the most unworkable deltas provide clues that lead to improvements.

Explore for hidden benefits in difficult deltas by asking yourself:

Why would someone suggest that?

How else can we achieve the same result?

What other information might I need to understand this?

If appropriate, you may want to use versions of these questions to introduce issues on the agendas of future meetings.

Tip #3

Suggest areas for deltas if none are offered. For example, if you were conducting a plus/delta on a meeting, you could ask:

How was the agenda?

What about the facilitation?

How about the logistics?

Tip #4

Ask questions to get the full benefit from this process.

The pluses are valuable because they identify things you want to continue. Invite pluses by asking:

How can we continue to achieve the same result?

What else can we do to achieve this result?

What is there about this that makes it favorable?

Tip #5

Evaluate pluses by challenging their durability. That is, ask yourself how soon will it be before the pluses become standard practice, imitated by the competition, or replaced by other priorities.

Variations on the process

Affinity Plus/Delta
Combine an affinity diagram process with the Plus/Delta. Set up two charts, one titled + and the other delta. Distribute Post-it™ Notes and marking pens to the participants. Ask them to write ideas and post them on the appropriate charts.

Confidential Complaint
If the issue is controversial and you think it will help, leave the room. Let members of the group facilitate the process.

Planned Improvement
Use this to plan the next version. For example, I led a group through a Plus/Delta after a fund raising event. We filled five charts with ideas. Then we gave the charts to next year's chair for the event and directed that we wanted to repeat the pluses and add the deltas.

Make success a cooperative project.

Reengineer
Use a Plus/Delta to plan the reengineering of a business. The process will identify what you should keep and what you need to change.

Example application

Continuous Improvement
I end most of my workshops on Effective Meetings with a Plus/Delta process. Through this I illustrate how the process works and I collect ideas on how to make the workshop more effective.

Then I study the suggestions. The pluses tell me what people liked, and the deltas challenge me to find new approaches. Even comments about things that could be the client's responsibility (e.g., snacks or directions to the meeting room) help me find ways to provide more successful programs. For example, based on deltas collected in the past, I recommend logistics that contribute to a successful workshop.

Key Ideas

▶ A Plus/Delta asks for ideas on what people liked and what they would like to do differently.

▶ Insist on deltas that show improvements instead of voice complaints.

▶ Show appreciation for all ideas, including those that seem impossible, wrong, or dumb. The most painful ideas may be the ones we need the most.

Chapter 9

Discussion

The Old Standard

What it is

This is an unstructured process where the participants exchange ideas on an issue.

Since this is similar to ordinary communication (through conversation) it is popular. It becomes inefficient when the focus drifts or a minority dominate.

It's almost a social activity.

Applications

Use this process when the group wants an independent exchange of ideas. A discussion can:

▶ Provide an unstructured exploration of options

▶ Survey reactions, needs, and opinions

▶ Allow the more aggressive participants opportunities to speak

▶ Provide an outlet for ideas that accumulated during a structured process

▶ Serve as a bridge between structured processes

Important point

How it works

The participants exchange ideas through group conversation.

The success of this process depends upon how it is administered. At its worst, a discussion begins with a vague question such as, *Well, what do you want to talk about?* Then some of the participants respond by playing games such as Look at Me or Ain't It Awful. The rest watch in quiet frustration.

At its best, a discussion can help people quickly explore options, survey viewpoints, or exchange ideas. Guide the process by asking questions and by questioning unrelated comments.

What it does

This process allows people to share ideas as they think of them.

What to expect

The more aggressive participants will speak first and most often. Focus on the issue may drift after a few minutes. Most of the participants will act as if this is normal.

Tip #1

If the group starts a discussion, let them know they chose this process by saying:

It seems we're holding a discussion on this issue.

Tip #2

Set a time limit. This prevents a discussion from taking over the entire meeting. You could say:

Let's discuss this for the next five minutes.

I can tell you want to talk about these results. Let's allot five minutes for the discussion.

Tip #3

Gently keep the group's focus on track. If the discussion wanders to unrelated topics, challenge this by saying:

How does that relate to our topic?

Is this what you want to be talking about?

Excuse me. We have two minutes left for this discussion and I wonder if we're covering the points we want to make.

Variation on the process

The Magic Mug

Use a speaking prop with the magical quality of allowing the holder to speak. A gavel, coffee mug, or other object of similar significance will work. This regulates the discussion by protecting the speaker from interruptions.

This variation has the disadvantage of becoming a power game. The speaker can exclude opposing views by talking for the entire meeting or by transferring the prop to members with supporting views. If this happens, you should control transfer of the prop.

Key Ideas

▶ A discussion is an unstructured conversation held by a group.

▶ Use this process with caution to gather general ideas.

▶ Apply a time limit to prevent discussions from using all the time allotted for the meeting.

Section 2
Sort the Harvest

I'm sure there's a decision in here somewhere.

Step 2:
Select Ideas

You just collected ideas with a structured process and now charts cover the walls. In total, they hold a mindboggling collection of intellectual whales and minnows, assets and liabilities, answers and puzzles.

The following process tools help you identify the best ideas. Depending upon the issue, best could mean easiest effort, lowest cost, most popular, faster gain, least destructive, or most influential.

These techniques are fast, easy, and fun. And most important, all reach decisions based on consensus, which promotes cooperation.

Chapter 10

Standard Voting

Aye, Nay

What it is

Participants make yes/no decisions by voting for or against issues.

Applications

Use this process for any issue with two sides.

How it works

This process is conducted according to the rules of parliamentary procedure (see Robert's Rules of Order, the official manual on parliamentary law). First someone proposes a decision by making a motion. Then someone seconds the motion, thereby showing at least two people support considering the issue further. After discussing the motion, the chairperson leads the group in voting. For example:

Chairperson: *It has been moved and seconded that starting next week we will wear red beanies on Fridays. All those in favor signify by saying 'Aye'.*

Five people say, *Aye.*

Everyone has used this type of voting.

Chairperson: *Those opposed, signify by saying 'Nay'.*

Two people say, *Nay.*

Chairperson: *The 'Ayes' have it. We will wear red beanies on Fridays starting next week.*

A less formal (and incomplete) version could sound like:

What about those beanies?

Five people shrug.

Okay, that's decided. Now, what's next?

However it goes (see Tip #1), the process begins with a statement of the issue, proceeds with a call for votes, and ends with an announcement of the result. It is simple, easy, and fast.

What it does
This process lets the majority approve or veto a proposal.

What to expect
It should follow the first script above. The chair calls for a vote, the participants respond, and the chair reports on the result.

Tip #1
Take the time to use a complete formal approach because it prevents misunderstandings. State the complete motion and ask for *Aye* and *Nay* votes specifically. This makes sure the participants know what they are voting for. Then report the result.

Tip #2

Keep the process simple. I witnessed a meeting where a group defeated their opposition with a superior knowledge of parliamentary procedure instead of with a majority vote.

The purpose of this process tool is to reach a fair decision, not to demonstrate a superior knowledge of parliamentary procedure.

Variations on the process

Collect votes by raising hands, calling roll, filling out ballots, or stepping across a line. The choice depends upon how close the vote is, requirements to document support, the importance of anonymity, and the need for drama.

Example application

All those in favor of reading further signify by raising your hand.

Those opposed, signify by raising their hand. (No one raises a hand.)

It's unanimous. We'll continue reading and learning how to hold fewer, shorter, more effective meetings.

Key Ideas

▶ Parliamentary procedure is a popular means of letting the majority approve or veto a proposal.

▶ To conduct standard voting, state the motion, call for the Ayes, call for the Nays, and report the result.

▶ Avoid shortcuts because they can create confusion.

Chapter 11

Dot Voting

Here Come the Dots!

What it is

This process helps participants select items from a list based on some criteria.

Applications

Use this process any time you want a group to choose two or more items from a list of candidates. This process can also help prioritize a list of candidates.

How it works

The following instructions apply to a collection of ideas on chart paper.

1) Count the number of choices.

2) Divide this number by three and round to the nearest integer. I often round up even if the fraction is a third because an extra choice makes people feel powerful.

I like dots.

3) Give each participant the number of dots (purchased from office supply stores) that you calculated.

Of course, the number of dots must be less than the total number of choices.

Instead of dots you can use push pins, Post-it™ Notes, initials, check marks, buttons, coins, or ballots.

4) The participants vote by placing dots (on the chart paper) next to the items they feel meet the criteria for the process.

Voting with dots follows these rules:

▶ Participants vote for their choices by placing one dot next to each choice.

▶ Participants must vote all their dots.

▶ Each participant is limited to the dots distributed for the decision. Participants may not borrow, sell, steal, donate, trade, remove, or relocate dots. They may not bring dots from home. They may not create counterfeit dots. (Expect that some people will seek creative ways to influence important decisions.)

5) After all the dots have been voted, count the dots for each item.

6) Rank the items according to the number of dots each received.

Check for wayward dots. A lost dot could change the decision.

What it does

This process determines which items best meet the criteria for the issue.

What to expect

Voting with dots is dynamic. It makes people leave their seats and move about to vote.

The participants place dots next to the items that they think meet the criteria. Some people will finish quickly, others will wait until most have voted before voting their dots.

If someone wants to change a vote, remove the old dot or draw a mark through it. Then give the person a new dot.

Tip #1

Choose dots that have a different color than the text on the charts. This makes it easy to count all the dots. A wayward dot could miss being counted because it looked like a period, written dot, or stray mark.

Tip #2

Group dots on the same side of the chart, close to the item to ensure that votes are tallied as intended. Stray dots could end up supporting someone else's ideas.

Tip #3

Clearly state the intent of the voting to ensure that everyone votes with the same understanding of the issue. For example you might say:

Vote for the locations that you like the most.

Vote for the candidates we should hire.

Important point

Vote for the strategies that will help us make the most money.

Emphasize key words (e.g., *most*) to make sure no one thinks *least*. It is amazing but true that people will hear what they are thinking more clearly than what you are saying.

Variations on the process

Roll Call Dots

Give each participant a different color dot or ask the participants to write their initials on their dots. This has the advantage of helping the participants identify their votes. It has the disadvantage of allowing participants to identify each other's votes.

Ballot Voting

Give each participant a ballot listing the choices. Each participant marks a third (or some fraction) of the choices. This variation has the following advantages:

▶ Participants vote with complete anonymity.

▶ It clearly shows the participant which choices were made (i.e., no confusion with other people's dots).

▶ It can be performed while sitting at a conference table or in a small room.

Its disadvantages include:

▶ It is less dynamic.

▶ Participants are unable to observe the result develop. They must wait until the ballots are tallied and the result reported.

▶ It takes more time. Someone has to prepare a ballot and then tally the votes.

Example application

How Can We ...?

•• ✔ Average idea

•••• ✔ Great idea

• ✔ Unpopular idea

•••••• ✔ Creative idea

✔ Harmful idea

The creative idea received the most dots.

Key Ideas

▶ Participants can prioritize a list of candidates by placing dots next to their choices. Give each person one third as many dots as candidates.

▶ Dot voting has the advantage of being a dynamic, group process.

Chapter 12

Weighted Dot Voting

More Control With Dots

What it is
This process helps participants select items from a list based on some criteria.

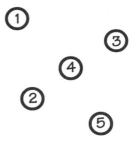

Applications
Use this process any time a group wants to choose two or more items from a list of candidates and they want some votes to count more than others. This process can also help prioritize a list of candidates.

How it works
1) Give each participant dots. If N equals the number of items, you can distribute N/3, N/2, or N dots. Distributing fewer dots forces participants to exclude low priority items instead of giving them low value votes.

2) The participants write numbers on their dots that represent the value of each vote. For example, five dots would receive 5 (first choice), 4, 3, 2, and 1 (last choice).

These dots have values.

3) The participants vote by placing their dots next to the items they prefer.

4) Add the numbers on the dots that were voted for each item. Results are scored in terms of the totals obtained for each item.

What it does
This process allows people to combine priorities with preferences.

What to expect
The dynamics of this process are the same as for N/3 Dot Voting, with one exception. A minority can dominate weighted voting if enough participants vote their highest value dots for the same items.

Tip #1
Let the group decide if they want to use Weighted Dot Voting. Then let them choose the parameters for the process.

Tip #2
Keep this process as simple as possible. Elaborate weighting systems require more effort to administer and can yield meaningless results.

Tip #3
Use different colors or shapes to signify different weights.

Important point

Variations on the process

Ultra-simple Weighting
Possibilities include:

▶ Half the dots are worth two points, the rest are worth one point.

▶ Each participant receives one dot worth two points, the rest are worth one point

Paper Ballot
The participants vote with a printed ballot.

Example application

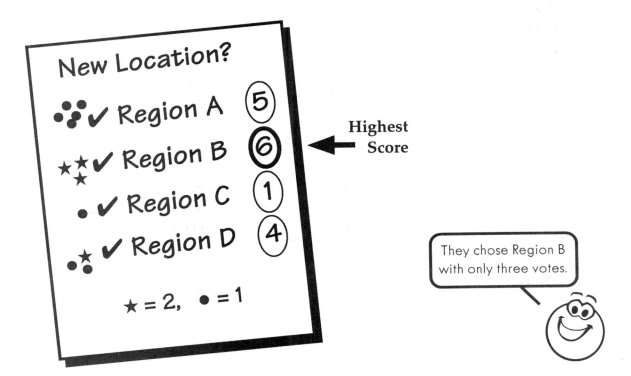

Key Ideas

▶ In weighted dot voting, the participants assign values to their dots to show the amount of preference they feel for their priorities.

▶ Keep the rules for this process simple to save time and avoid meaningless results.

Chapter 13

Fail Safe Voting

Prevent Harmful Decisions

What it is

This process helps participants select and veto candidate items. It has the advantage of helping the group reach win/win decisions.

Applications

Use this process any time a group wants to choose items from a list of controversial candidates. This process can also help prioritize a list of candidates.

How it works

1) Give each participant as many dots as there are items. You can also use small labels or Post-it™ Notes.

2) The participants vote for each item indicating one of the following levels of support:

▶ Enthusiastic: like the item and will volunteer to implement it. Mark a 3 on the dot.

▶ Moderate: favor the item and will speak positively about it. Mark a 2 on the dot.

I need this.

▶ Minimal: accept the item and will tolerate it until a better one appears. Mark a 1 on the dot.

▶ Opposed: reject the item and will resist or even sabotage it. Mark an **X** on the dot.

3) Add the total numbers voted for each item. Any item receiving an **X** is set aside. The totals show support for the items.

4) Rejected items may require further evaluation. If, for example, a popular item is rejected, then the participants must resolve this by asking:

How can we meet our needs without it?

How can we change the item so it becomes acceptable to everyone?

How is this harmful to the person who rejected it?

False compliance

What it does

This process leads to results that are acceptable for everyone. Thus, it protects the minority from being forced to accept harmful decisions.

It also avoids false compliance, which occurs when people feel forced into decisions that they have no intention of honoring.

What to expect

As before, the group will usually select the most popular items. This process becomes challenging, however, when someone rejects a popular item. Participants will ask, *How can you reject that?*

A philosophical thought

Seeking win/win solutions requires overcoming difficult challenges and perhaps making painful sacrifices. The results are worth the effort. The members of a win/win culture feel more respect, support, and trust for the organization and its leaders.

In contrast, win/lose options become self-defeating because:

▶ Win/lose decisions, though beneficial for some, reduce the productivity of those who lose.

▶ Opponents convert win/lose decisions into lose/lose situations through resistance or sabotage.

▶ A win/lose culture fosters predatory practices that damage productivity.

Tip #1

If someone rejects an option, assume the person has a valid reason. Avoid forceful attempts to change the person's mind. Instead, ask open questions to understand the reasons for the rejection and seek alternatives. This dialogue often leads to a win/win solution.

Important point

Tip #2

Use large dots that permit clear writing of numbers and (if agreed upon) initials.

Tip #3

Depending upon the issue, it may be more effective to deal with a rejected option by asking a subcommittee to find an equitable resolution.

Variations on the process

It's My Vote
The participants write their initials on votes that reject an option. This trades anonymity for an open dialogue to understand rejection and find equitable resolution.

Secret Ballot
The participants vote with a printed ballot. Any rejection must be accompanied by an explanation and proposed alternatives.

Key Ideas
▶ Fail Safe Voting protects the minority from being hurt by popular but destructive decisions.

▶ Conduct a fail safe voting by including a veto option in weighted dot voting. Then deal with rejected popular options by seeking win/win alternatives.

▶ A rejection may require further consideration to understand its basis and to find equitable resolution.

Chapter 14

Ranking

Line up the Candidates

What it is
This process helps a group prioritize a list of options.

Applications
Use this process when a group wants to prioritize a complete list of options. It works best with at least 3 and less than 12 items. With more than 12 items it can take a long time.

How it works
1) Write each option on a Post-it™ Note (an index card or other note paper will work).

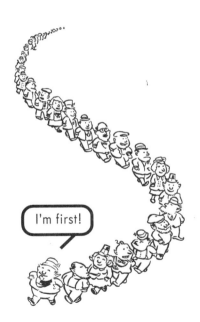

I'm first!

2) Place the Post-it™ Notes in a column on a chart paper or other surface.

3) Point to the first two Notes and ask, *Do you like the first option more than the second?* If the group agrees, leave the Notes where they are. If the group likes the second option more, then move the second Note above the first.

4) Point to the second and third Notes and ask, *Do you like the second option more than the third?* If the group agrees, leave the Notes where they are and move to step 5. If the group likes the third option more, then exchange the positions for the two Notes. Now repeat step #3 for the Note in first place and the Note that you moved into second place.

5) Continue comparing pairs, until the group agrees on the relative ranking of all the candidates.

What it does
This process ranks options according to the group's priorities.

What to expect
If the choices are easy, the process proceeds quickly. You may feel challenged to move the Notes fast enough to keep up with the group. If, however, the choices are difficult, you can expect active discussion over every move.

Tip #1
Move the Notes deliberately, so everyone sees the change. If you move the Notes too quickly the process looks like the infamous shell game.

Tip #2
Use a consistent pattern when asking the group to choose. For example, you could say:

Do you like the second option more than the third? (by actual position)

Important point

Do you like the top option more than the bottom? (by relative position)

Do you like Pat Smith more than Chris Brown? (by option)

Example application

Ask: Is **X** better than **Y**?

Decide: **X** is better than **Y**.

Move: None

If **X** is better than **Y**, then it stays on top.

Ask: Is **Y** better than **Z**?

Decide: **Z** is better than **Y**.

Move: Place **Z** above **Y**.

So, **Z** moves above **Y** and below **X**.

Ask: Is **X** better than **Z**?

Decide: **Z** is better than **X**.

Move: Place **Z** above **X**.

Now **Z** moves above **X**.

Final Position

All done!

Key Ideas

▶ Use movable Notes to help a group prioritize a list of options. Arrange the Notes in a column, ask for comparisons between pairs, and change positions of the Notes, putting the preferred option on top.

▶ Conduct the steps deliberately so the participants can follow what you are doing.

Section 3
Results

Step 3:
Make Plans

This step justifies holding a meeting. Now, you convert the consensus reached on the ideas into action items.

Chapter 15

Action Items
Converting Ideas Into Reality

Four Elements
The payoff in a meeting occurs when you convert ideas into action items. At this point you should have collected ideas and reached consensus on the most important idea.

An action item has four elements.

1) Task

2) Who

3) Completion Date

4) Resources

1) Task
Start by writing **Action Item** at the top of a fresh chart page. Under this, write the first element, **Task**. Then point to the idea that the group selected for action and confirm their decision by asking:

Is this our next step?

Is this what we want to do?

It seems we chose <idea>. Is that right?

If the group agrees, write that idea on the chart. This identifies the idea as the task for the action item.

2) Who

Then write **Who** on the chart and ask for a volunteer to carry out the idea. For example, you could ask:

Who wants to take responsibility for <action>?

Who's responsible for this <type of work>?

Who wants to do this?

Write the volunteer's name on the chart and confirm if the group agrees. In some situations the "volunteer" may be selected by the participants.

3) Completion Date

Next write **Completion Date** on the chart and ask the volunteer:

When do you expect to finish?

What is your completion date?

Sometimes the volunteer will need to plan before committing to a completion date. When this happens ask the volunteer to estimate completion dates for the planning process. For example, ask:

When do you expect to complete a schedule?

When will the first step be completed?

Write that date on the chart followed by the action it represents (e.g., hold planning meeting, define scope of work, prepare time line). Then ask the participants if this schedule meets their needs and expectations. If they disagree, you need to resolve that in the meeting.

4) Resources

Last, write **Resources** on the chart and ask the volunteer to estimate the amount of labor, time, and money needed to complete the task. Write this information on the chart and ask the group if these expenditures agree with their expectations.

This approach goes beyond defining action items: it builds accountability into the results. Elements 3) and 4) provide information that you can use to measure progress on the action item. For example, you can check if the planning meeting occurred when proposed.

When you define action items during the meeting you ensure that everyone understands and supports the scope of their implementation. This eliminates costly misunderstandings.

For example, suppose the group had decided to build a new office, expecting a single room hut. But the volunteer planned to build a magnificent brick building. Obviously, it would help to uncover and resolve this difference as soon as possible.

Everyone Else   Volunteer

Key Ideas

▶ Define action items by obtaining answers to four questions.

1) What is the task?

2) Who will be responsible for it?

3) When will the task be completed?

4) What resources (labor, time, and materials) will be used?

▶ Make sure the group agrees with all parts of the action item. Then document this information in the minutes.

Section 4
Leadership

Create Success

Leading a meeting is a complex task. It requires attention, confidence, courage, creativity, detachment, diplomacy, empathy, flexibility, focus, humor, sensitivity, wits, and toughness.

After reading the above sentence some people will want to close this book. They'll think, *That applies only to the person who runs the meeting.*

In reality, a meeting can be led from any chair in the room. That means an unprepared chairperson could become a participant in someone else's meeting.

The following techniques will make you a more effective chairperson, facilitator, or participant.

Chapter 16

The Agenda
Start by Knowing the Plan

Why Meetings Fail

Lack of an agenda is the number one reason for failed meetings. An agenda is essential because it puts you in control of the meeting. If you want to distinguish yourself as a leader by conducting effective meetings, you will prepare an agenda. Without an agenda, your meetings become journeys without a map.

Parts of an Agenda

A complete agenda has four parts. When planning an agenda, remember **G O A L S**.

G = Goals

Goals ensure success by defining the results of a meeting. They:

▶ Make sure everyone works on the same thing

▶ Tell the chair what to request

▶ Tell the participants what to do

▶ Help determine when the task is complete

When planning goals, use the popular acronym SMART. Notice how it improves the following goals.

S = Specific (e.g., *Plan a job interview for the new sales position*, instead of job candidate)

M = Measurable (e.g., *Develop three strategies to increase sales by 5%*, instead of make more money)

A = Achievable (e.g., *Reduce production waste by 4%*, instead of eliminate pollution)

R = Relevant (e.g., *Plan next year's inventory*, instead of my fishing trip)

T = Time (i.e., the time allotted for each activity)

Examples of effective goals for meetings are:

▶ Identify 3 things we can do to reduce waste on Unit #5 in the next 20 minutes.

▶ Identify and assign responsibilities for the job interview this Friday, in the next 15 minutes.

▶ Create a name for the new laptop computer, in the next 20 minutes.

▶ Identify the causes of reduced sales in Region #3, in the next 20 minutes.

▶ Prepare a draft of a mission statement for the marketing department, in the next hour.

Goals are critically important. As a chairperson you have to know what you want in order to ask for it. As a participant, you have to know what you are doing in order to tell when you have finished.

If you have no goals, you may as well take your time.

O = Outcomes

Outcomes show paths to solutions.

I'll admit that outcomes are often more conceptual than factual. Nevertheless, they serve to show why we are holding the meeting by describing the benefits of achieving the goals. Outcomes can also help people find creative solutions by describing the characteristics of the ideal result.

They address:

What will happen?

▶ We will finish the year within our budget.

▶ We will keep our inventory up to date.

▶ We will stay in business.

What will people say?

▶ Our boss will congratulate us.

▶ Our competition will be stunned.

▶ The owner will smile.

What will we feel?

▶ We will feel proud of ourselves.

▶ We will feel relieved.

▶ We will feel satisfaction.

What will we see?

▶ We will see a shining new unit that works.

▶ We will see our picture in the annual report.

▶ We will see an increase in pay.

L = List of Activities

The list of activities is a blueprint for a successful meeting. It tells 1) what will happen, 2) who is responsible for each activity, and 3) the schedule of activities. For example, here is a list of activities for a meeting that starts at 9 o'clock.

Notice that if people arrive 5 minutes late they're still on time.

8:55	Arrive	Everyone
9:00	Open meeting, review goals	Chair
9:02	Collect ideas to increase sales (Brainstorm)	Facilitator
9:08	Select 3 best ideas (Dot Vote)	Everyone
9:12	Plan action on 3 best ideas	Everyone
9:28	Review results	Chair
9:30	Adjourn	Chair

This list completely describes the meeting's activities. And notice that the arrival time is scheduled on the agenda.

L = Logistics

Logistics help everyone succeed at a meeting by telling them how to prepare and what to bring. When participants travel, logistics can include information on lodging, restaurants, local travel directions (maps), appropriate clothes, weather conditions, activities for family members, cultural guidelines, entertainment, public resources, and medical services.

S = Strategy

Preparing an agenda also involves planning strategies that ensure a successful meeting. This includes researching the issues and arranging for success.

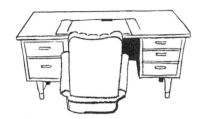

Successful meetings start here.

Determine who supports the issues and learn why. Meet with the opponents and listen to their arguments. In both cases, listen to understand rather than to change. At this point you want to learn why people feel the way they do. You will also win respect from everyone for showing a sincere interest in their views.

Uncover obstacles to progress and resolve them before the meeting. This can include uncomfortable room conditions, inconvenient starting times, absent participants, missing materials, faulty equipment, and unprepared presenters.

Check the emotional climate. Sometimes a major event leaves people too upset to focus on the issues. If that is the case, reschedule the meeting.

What to do with an agenda

Distribute the agenda to the participants far enough in advance of the meeting so they can prepare for the meeting.

This may seem obvious, and yet many meeting organizers bring the agenda to the meeting. This leaves the participants no time to research, study, or think about the issues. That results in an efficient meeting.

Tip #1

Schedule a break at least every hour. People need it.

Tip #2

If you are the chairperson, ask the facilitator to prepare the agenda.

Tip #3

Prepare the agenda with the help of key participants. They can identify the most important issues, select key participants, and plan activities.

Tip #4

Tell the participants how to prepare in the agenda. For example you could ask the participants to read documents, forecast expenses, or collect ideas.

▼▼▼▼▼▼

Key Ideas

Remember, you should prepare agendas only for the meetings you want to succeed.

▶ The success of a meeting depends upon planning. An agenda communicates your plans to the participants. The agenda should be sent to the participants before the meeting.

▶ An agenda should contain **Goals, Outcomes, Activities,** and **Logistics.** Add an **S** for the strategies that ensure success and we have the acronym **G O A L S**.

▶ The best goals are **Specific, Measurable, Achievable,** and **Relevant.** They specify deadlines (**Time**).

Chapter 17

Encourage Success

Create a Safe Environment

The Ideal Meeting

A productive meeting occurs when the participants feel free to explore new ideas, speak openly, and ask questions. They need to believe their ideas are significant steps in a staircase that the group is building toward a successful future. They need to trust that all their contributions are appreciated, including those that prove untenable.

Creative Thinking Allowed

This may sound like an impossible fantasy because real life is filled with tension, conflict, and adversity.

The key is the source of adversity. If it comes from outside in the form of looming competition, rampaging change, or impending bankruptcy then it brings people together. If, however, it comes from within in the form of criticism, disrespect, or plagiarism then it shuts down thinking.

As a leader, you want to make sure the governing forces move people toward your goals instead of

Important point

away from them. The following actions help create a safe, productive environment.

Tell people they're important

People contribute more when their ideas are appreciated. They think more freely when they feel important. They accept change more readily when they feel secure. As a facilitator, you can supercharge people's minds by appreciating their ideas. For example, you can open a meeting by saying:

I believe all your ideas are important.

I invited you to this meeting because I value your ideas.

Everyone here is an expert on some part of this issue and I need your help.

Although we may have different views on this issue, I know we can find equitable solutions by working as a team.

Everyone here is an important person who has valuable ideas.

These complimentary statements assure people that you respect them and their ideas.

Set Ground Rules

Call them rules, laws, norms, instructions, or cultural expectations. They all serve the same purpose–to define a consistent culture.

Meetings work better when everyone knows and follows the same set of rules.

The following ground rules are used by many organizations.

Ground Rules Prevent Problems

▶ Work as a team

▶ No rank in the room

▶ One speaker at a time

▶ Be an active listener

▶ Focus on the issue

▶ Respect others

▶ Suspend judgment

▶ Allow curiosity, discovery

▶ Participate freely when appropriate

▶ Maintain confidentiality

You may want to modify this list to suit your needs. If you do, however, be sure that you gain everyone's agreement on the new list.

Some facilitators begin a meeting by showing the ground rules and saying, *These are the ground rules for our meeting. Do we agree to follow them?*

Usually everyone replies, *Yes.*

There is value in checking for agreement on the ground rules. For example, if someone were to say, *No! I want to be rude, abusive, and insult people,* then you can explore if the other participants support such behavior.

Ground rules also keep a meeting on track. If the group's behavior strays, you can remind them, *We agreed to follow these rules.*

Smile

This easy, inexpensive activity signals acceptance and confidence. Everyone can smile. The impact works wonders.

Of course, your smile must be genuine, relaxed, and friendly. We have all seen smiles that could freeze lava. Your smile should convey, *This is a safe place.*

Key Ideas

▶ A safe environment helps people work at their creative best.

▶ You can create a safe (and productive environment) by affirming people's importance, setting ground rules, and acting pleasant.

Chapter 18

Rise Above Challenges

Maintain the Environment

The Trap

Some leaders lose people's trust because they fall in the trap of, *Believe what I say, not what I do.* For example, a chairperson may ask the participants to support each other in working toward a solution, and then react with hostility when challenged with new ideas.

When this happens, the participants become cautious. They shut down their creativity and cooperation. They become passive robots interested in finding the right answers instead of the best solutions. As a result the meeting becomes a waste of time.

Thus you want your responses to ideas and activities in the meeting to support the positive environment that you started. As you must expect, some situations will make this especially challenging. You will hear ideas and witness behavior that bothers you. If you are the facilitator, the group may challenge your role or make decisions that you dislike.

So that's why some people lose control of their meetings.

First, realize that you can accept something and still disagree with it. Acceptance means that we acknowledge without arguing, complaining, or fighting back.

How you respond to disagreeable activities depends upon your role in the meeting. If you are a participant, then it is your responsibility to speak up. If, however, you are the facilitator, then your response must help the group reach the best result.

During a meeting you may witness amazing ideas and amazing attacks. Here is how to deal with each.

Amazing Ideas

Amazing ideas include anything that seems awful, bad, terrible, unfounded, impossible, stupid, dangerous, destructive, backward, progressive, shallow, thoughtless, insulting, unkind, unworkable, expensive, radical, unconventional, liberal, conservative, illegal, crazy, and original. Sometimes an idea sounds amazing because the other person thinks differently. Other times the idea is truly amazing.

If someone offers an amazing idea during an Idea Harvest, simply write the idea on the chart and continue. If you feel like doing so, you could acknowledge the person by saying *Okay* or *Thanks*. At this stage of a meeting, amazing ideas are relatively harmless because the participants will deal with them later.

Also, amazing ideas can prove valuable because:

▶ They stir the creativity of other participants, leading to better ideas.

▶ They allow people to ventilate discontent, which then frees them to focus on solutions.

▶ They allow people to test your leadership. If you accept a sacrificial, dumb idea, then they feel safe to share a truly novel (and valuable) idea.

Amazing Attacks

If someone offers a disagreeable idea that requires a response, you have many options. Notice that all of these use verbal parallels to the martial arts. That is, they honor the opponent and then convert the opponent's energy into a positive force.

You can:

1) Acknowledge the idea and continue. For example, you could say:

Acknowledge and continue

Thank you for that insight.

I appreciate your remark.

Thank you for that viewpoint.

After replying, look at someone else and wait for the next idea. This directs control away from the person who attacked and toward others in the meeting.

The unspoken words behind this approach are: *I heard the comment and chose to ignore it.* If the disagreeable idea was important someone else will keep it alive. Then you will have to exercise other approaches.

2) Acknowledge differences of opinion and invite discussion to understand and resolve them by saying:

Accept the differences

We seem to see this differently. Let's explore our differences.

We seem to feel differently about this. Let's explore those differences.

We seem to have different expectations. Let's explore those differences.

An open, candid response shows you have the confidence and courage to rise above disagreements. In addition, sometimes a disagreeable idea is actually a poorly worded warning, suggestion, or call for help. If you turn these situations into solutions you will win respect from others.

Focus on a question that you want to answer

3) Rephrase the idea in a positive way. To do this, first guess the rationale behind the idea and then build your response around that.

What I think you're saying is you disagree with my position on this issue.

What I think you want is a different approach to our program.

Notice that these replies maintain open, positive communication while retaining dignity. If fact, dignified replies leave insulting behavior with the heckler.

Most insults are bait wrapped around a sharp hook. If you swallow the bait, you become caught in a devastating argument, which is what the heckler wants. Instead, move the conversation to a more productive issue where you can identify and fix the conflict.

4) Seek clarification. Here, you assume additional information would help. So, you could say:

Thank you. Now, how would we do that?

Interesting. Now, what would be the advantages of that?

Thank you. Now, what would happen if we did that?

Make sure you both understand the issue

5) Involve the other participants. Direct the issue to the group by asking questions, such as:

How do you feel about this? (This tests the group's reaction to the amazing idea.)

How would this affect the rest of you? (This explores the validity of the idea with those most affected by it.)

Does anyone else share that view? (This checks if others agree. Use this reply with caution because you want to avoid starting a popularity contest.)

Okay, what do you want to do next? (This asks the group for direction on the next step. Recall a facilitator helps a group find solutions to their problems.)

Recruit help

6) Suggest another time to discuss the issue by saying:

This is an important issue that we need to discuss. Rather than use our time today, I suggest we work on it tomorrow in my office at ten.

That's a complex issue, which I think we need to put on the agenda for our next meeting.

That sounds like a personal issue, and I think we should discuss it further in private. Let's meet in my office tomorrow at ten.

Pick a time when you can discuss the issue without an audience

Some disagreements require solutions that exceed the scope, resources, or time available in a meeting. And some disagreements lose their energy when dealt with in private, without an audience. Thus the best approach may be to adjourn, deal with the issue, and schedule another meeting.

Good news about safe environments.

Safe environments encourage open examination of all ideas, including those that disturb you. Thus, other participants may defend you by finding flaws, stating objections, and offering counterproposals to amazing ideas.

Key Ideas

▶ Maintain a positive environment by rising above disagreeable ideas and activities.

▶ Realize you can accept without agreeing.

▶ Most amazing ideas will either lead to useful ideas or disappear during later stages of the meeting.

▶ Deal with attacks by converting the issue into a positive statement that you can answer or by deferring the issue until a more appropriate time.

Chapter 19

Facilitation

Guide the Process

An Important Difference

The facilitator serves a unique role in a meeting. While the participants work to build solutions, the facilitator works to build processes that lead to solutions. This responsibility requires different actions driven by a different perspective.

In the course of a meeting the facilitator will use the techniques described in this book. That is, the facilitator will select an appropriate process (Chapters 2-15), start the dialogue with questions (Chapter 1), and maintain progress toward equitable results (Chapters 17-22). This makes facilitation a full time job.

Thus, if you plan to facilitate your meeting (i.e., when you are the chairperson), realize that this removes you from acting as a participant. The keys to successful facilitation are detachment and focus.

This can be a challenge.

Detachment

Sometimes you will feel an emotional investment in the meeting. You will want the best ideas and the

Even though you may want to help, a facilitator must remember it's the participants' problem.

people supporting them to succeed. Thus, you may feel tempted to participate in the processes.

When this temptation arises your response should be absolute, complete, and total detachment.

You will be most effective as a facilitator when you:

▶ Stay out of the process (even if it seems like fun)

▶ Avoid taking sides (even if you favor one view)

▶ Speak diplomatically (even if people attack you)

▶ Communicate positively (even if everyone else is negative)

▶ Avoid fixing people (even if they appear to need it)

▶ Respect everyone (even if people express uncomfortable values)

▶ Act with courage (even if you feel fear)

▶ Remain calm (even if everyone else acts crazy)

An Exception

I discourage facilitators from participating in a meeting. If you must, however, you should realize:

Potential Consequences - Ouch

▶ You risk losing control of the meeting.

▶ You could lead the group to a different result than they would have found on their own. Then you share responsibility for it.

▶ You may become involved in an argument.

▶ You may add energy to a disagreement.

▶ You risk showing support for one viewpoint, which will destroy your credibility as a neutral facilitator.

▶ You may be unable to resume being the facilitator.

Potential Consequences - Good

▶ You may contribute valuable information.

How to do it

If you want to be a part-time participant:

1) Announce that you want to change roles by saying:

I have an idea and want to participate. Is that okay?

I noticed something. Is it okay if I become a participant to tell you about it?

It better be an incredibly wonderful contribution

If the participants decline your offer to participate, thank them and continue as facilitator. Caution: forcing an idea on the group leads to the negative (ouch!) consequences listed above.

2) Acknowledge the group's approval of your participation. Say *Thank you,* and take a step to the side. This change in position signals that you changed roles.

3) Offer your idea clearly and concisely. Long-winded statements risk negative consequences (see above).

4) Immediately return to the role of facilitator. Say *That ends my contribution. Now I'm returning to the role of facilitator.* Then step back to where you were standing because this physically signals you have returned to your original role as facilitator.

Focus

Facilitation requires absolute focus on the progress of the meeting. Evaluate each step for its contribution to results by asking yourself:

Where is this going?

Are the activities consistent with the goals for the meeting?

Are the participants working together?

Is the use of time consistent with the value of the result?

How is the energy in the room affecting the process?

Are hidden agendas at work here?

How do they feel about this?

What must I do to keep the meeting focused, fair, and productive?

Key Ideas

▶ Facilitation is a full time job. If you decide to facilitate your meeting, realize that this removes you from being a participant.

▶ A facilitator focuses on the process for progress toward results.

▶ Facilitators remain detached from the issues, the personalities, and the politics in a meeting. Attempts to become involved can destroy productivity.

Chapter 20

Uh Oh!

When Problems Appear

Expect Surprises

Despite your best efforts some people will lapse into unproductive behavior. Left alone, this undermines everyone's productivity and makes it more difficult to facilitate the meeting.

If unproductive behavior occurs, there are three rules: be gentle, be polite, be firm.

Use a Gentle Touch

I realize it may feel tempting to intervene with force. Direct confrontation such as admonitions (*Don't be a jerk!*), directions (*Hey you, pay attention!*), and insults (*That's stupid!*), seem efficient. Indirect attacks such as sarcasm (*Here's another question from the department with all the answers*), trick questions (*What kind of idiot would do that?*), and indifference (*Hummffff!*) seem clever. After all, they work in sitcoms.

Such attacks, however, hurt the target, create resentment, and reduce cooperation. They also show the other participants that you will punish. That instills caution and ultimately reduces everyone's productivity in your meeting.

In contrast, people find a gentle approach more appealing and convincing. You will also find it easier to apply.

It's a fact: we judge others by what we notice; they judge themselves by what they intend.

A gentle approach is safer, too, because initial observations can be misleading. Often additional facts exist that can change our perception of a situation. For example, in one workshop a participant seemed to be sleeping during most of my presentation. I wondered if the person was unmotivated. Later I learned the person was ill and had made a special effort to attend. If I had lashed out with criticism I would have created a big embarrassment for myself.

When problems occur it is essential that you maintain self-esteem while restoring productivity. This keeps the other person on your team and avoids a counter-attack, which can destroy a meeting. It also wins respect from the other participants in the meeting.

Valuable Tip
Apply the Platinum Rule. Treat the other person the way the person would want to be treated.

General Approach
Use the following general steps to deal with unproductive behavior in meetings. (Specific responses to the most common disruptions follow in Chapter 22.)

Step 1: Acknowledge the situation

This seemingly obvious step is important because it brings the behavior into the open where you can deal with it. The alternative is to ignore the behavior, but this indirectly endorses it. And that guarantees the behavior will continue.

In addition, people who ignore obvious problems appear like inattentive fools. It's like having a bird sit on your head while pretending everything is normal. The group sees the bird and wonders if you know about it. When you acknowledge the situation, you end illusions that such behavior is normal and set the stage for the next step.

State the facts by saying:

We have more than one conversation now.

We seem to have drifted from our topic.

We seem to disagree on this issue.

Step 2: Ask the group for help

A facilitator facilitates everything in a meeting, including the culture. Thus, deal with problems by talking to the group instead of to the source of the problem. For example, look at the group and say:

What do you want to work on next?

Could we have one conversation at a time?

How does this relate to the issue we're discussing?

We agreed to respect each other.

How important is this?

Who would like to be on a subcommittee to analyze alternatives?

Statements like these use the leverage of group pressure to correct unproductive behavior. They also keep you above the nasty mechanics of enforcing rules.

Remember, it is far easier to let a group determine its culture than to impose one.

Key Ideas

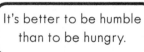

▶ Deal with difficult behavior diplomatically. Your perception of the situation may be incomplete or different from the other person's. And, in any case, you want to preserve everyone's self-esteem.

▶ There are two basic steps to correcting group behavior: 1) Acknowledge what is happening and 2) Ask the group for help.

Chapter 21

Escaping Dead Ends

When You Need a Way Out

Two Trump Cards

You applied the two basic steps to deal with a problem and it continued. So, now what do you do?

There are two trump cards you can play if a meeting becomes unmanageable. Of course, these actions need to be used with discretion. Otherwise, you will create a new unmanageable game.

Action #1: Call a break

Sometimes the best response to a problem is to detach from it. That may be the case when you need tranquility to consider options, safety to calm down, or privacy to coach someone.

Call a break by saying:

We seem to be at an impasse and the best thing we can do now is take a break.

We need to rest. Let's take a break.

We're stuck. Let's take a break.

Then use the break to improve the situation. You may want to:

Restore your calm

You have to help yourself before you can help others.

Sometimes the events in a meeting will frazzle your feelings. If you feel ready to scream, cry, run, or fight, use the break to heal your spirit.

First, leave the meeting physically and mentally. Find a private place such as your office, a stairwell, or the rest room. Take deep breaths, close your eyes, and relax. You may want to wash your face, take a walk, or climb stairs.

Then clear all thoughts about the meeting. Let your mind travel to a favorite memory or just fill with nothing. Repeat positive affirmations, such as:

I am okay.

I can handle this.

Let yourself fill with energy. Put aside hurt feelings. Build a calm, solid, professional frame of mind before you return to the meeting. You may also want to consider solutions that put the meeting back on track after the break.

Consider solutions

Use what you know to find a plan.

If you called a break to escape from a dilemma, you will need a plan for dealing with it before you return. Find a quiet place where you can think and take a moment to relax.

I recommend using private versions of the process tools to explore options. For example, you can conduct a personal brainstorm. Begin by writing a description of the dilemma as a question. For example, if you called a break because the meeting had zoomed out of control, you might write, *How can I regain control of the meeting?* If a disagreement blocked progress, you could write, *What's keeping us from agreeing on this issue?*

Then write answers to the question. Think openly, write quickly, and allow possibilities. When you finish, review the list to check if new options appear and select the most workable ideas.

Writing a list is a powerful way to find solutions. It helps you clarify the nature of the problem and collect possibilities.

You can also consider options with the help of other people. Just avoid starting a second meeting during the break. This could appear like subterfuge to the rest of the group and make you late returning to the meeting.

Meet privately
You can use a break to talk privately with the people you think are obstructing progress. Before you begin, however, take a moment to plan your approach.

Sometimes a private meeting helps.

Step #1. First decide what result you want (information or cooperation) and second consider if a private meeting is the best way to achieve it. In some situations it may be more effective to facilitate a group solution in the meeting than to obtain one privately.

You have to know your lines before you go on stage.

Step #2. Plan the conversation. Put yourself in the other person's position and imagine how that person might react to your opening statements. When we feel upset, we may want to tie our message to a flaming dart. Your intent, however, is to improve relationships so you can restore productivity in your meeting.

You will succeed best when you listen empathically and assert gently (see important caution about assertions below). This helps you gain information, soothe feelings, build rapport, and ease fears.

Step #3a. Gain information by inviting comments with positive validations, such as:

You seem to have a lot of experience with this system.

I'm impressed by your energy for this issue.

You seem to know a lot about the office in Region 6.

Or you ask friendly open-ended questions, such as:

I wonder what happened the last time you installed one of these.

What do you think causes people to feel that way?

How have your staff handled such orders in the past?

When finished, thank the person for talking with you, even if you dislike the information that you gained. It helps build rapport.

Then plan how this information will help you facilitate the meeting. For example, you may want to:

▶ Suggest changing the agenda to apply a process tool that leads to solutions in this situation.

▶ Guide the discussion toward people who can add to, verify, explain, or refute the new information.

▶ Adjourn so major differences can be resolved.

Step #3b. If you plan to ask for cooperation, you must first ask yourself the following important question:

Is a positive outcome possible?

Important point

Proceed only when your answer is an emphatic yes. If you feel any doubt, you are better off keeping silent. And if you feel moved to dispel that doubt because of charity, recall the story about Androcles and the Lion. It's a fable. In the real world, Androcles would have reached for his last thorn.

When you ask for cooperation make sure you send a positive message. This means you avoid accusations (*Only a dope would do that*), implied motives (*Are you trying to ruin the meeting?*), insults (*Hey, goof ball!*) threats (*Shape up or ship out*), trick questions (*Just what do you think you're doing?*), or verbal barbs (*It should be easy for someone with your intelligence to figure this out*).

Important point

Cunning, clever, or cute messages always backfire because they trigger defensive reactions instead of cooperative participation.

In addition, it is very important to speak with a pleasant, neutral voice. If you convey even a hint of anger or irritation the other person will hear that more clearly than your words. That can start an argument instead of win cooperation.

Sometimes in my workshops someone will propose derisive feedback. When I suggest positive statements are more effective, the person will say, *But I'd want to be told that way.*

If insults helped people improve, we would have fixed all human problems long ago.

Use the following script to ask for cooperation:

When .... (state the facts)

That .... (state the consequences)

And .... I feel (tell how you feel)

So, I want .... (tell what you want)

Is that okay? (ask for a commitment to change)

This entire message can be delivered with one or two breaths. It may go like this:

When you arrive late that wastes our time and I feel upset with that. So I want you to arrive on time. Is that okay?

When you call people names that causes them to stop contributing and I feel bad about that. So I want you to be polite. Is that okay?

When you carry on side conversations that distracts other participants and I feel bad that our meeting becomes unproductive. So I want you to share your ideas with everyone. Is that okay?

Notice these are clean statements. They simply state the facts, describe consequences, and ask for change.

Tip #1

Write out the message before you deliver it. This helps choose the right words and eliminate hostility. Then rehearse the message, either silently to yourself or with a trusted friend. That will help you say exactly what you want the way you want to say it.

Tip #2

Speak pleasantly with an even tone of voice. Requests for cooperation fail when spoken with sarcasm or screamed with rage.

Action #2: End the meeting

This is the ultimate trump card. Play it when you reach an impasse by saying:

We seem to be stuck and the best thing we can do is adjourn. We'll continue the meeting after we figure out how to resolve this.

We need to work on this outside the meeting. Let's adjourn and continue later.

We're stuck. Let's adjourn and finish later.

A meeting is a vehicle. When it wrecks, leave it.

Time to adjourn.

Of course, adjourning a meeting is like calling a long break. The situation that made it necessary to adjourn still exists. The work that you started remains unfinished. And the participants will wonder what happens next.

This means you will most likely have to call another meeting to finish the meeting you adjourned. Use the time between these meetings to improve the situation. Heal your spirit, plan solutions, revise the agenda, and (if appropriate) meet privately with key participants.

Key Ideas

▶ If a meeting zooms out of control, you can call a break or adjourn.

▶ Use this time to calm your feelings, plan solutions, or speak with the people causing the disruption.

▶ Request information and build rapport with positive validations and friendly questions.

▶ Offer coaching only if it can lead to a positive outcome.

▶ Coach privately with the script: *When ....* (state the facts), *That ....* (state the consequences), *And .... I feel* (tell how you feel), *So, I want ....* (tell what you want), *Is that okay?* (ask for a commitment to change).

Chapter 22

Difficult Behaviors

Situations That Stall Progress

An Important Limitation

The following sections show responses to the most common types of disruptive behavior. Of course, given the breadth of human creativity, other truly extraordinary situations may arise. For example, what do you do if the quiet manager on the third floor arrives wearing a chicken suit, throwing rotten eggs? Common sense suggests: call security and dodge the eggs. Your instincts and variations of the following responses will help you deal with the unexpected. And remember, as a last resort, you can always call a break or adjourn.

These responses bring most meetings back on track.

Situation: Multiple Conversations

This is the most common form of unproductive behavior. When someone begins a side conversation, at least two people leave the meeting—the talker and the talker's neighbor. If allowed to continue, side conversations grow like weeds until they take over

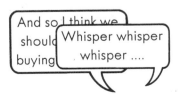

Side conversations make it hard for us to listen.

the meeting. Thus, you want to stop them as soon as they start.

Response: Ask for cooperation

The easiest approach is to ask the group for cooperation. Look at the middle of the group (instead of at the talker) and say:

Excuse me. I'm having difficulty hearing what [contributing participant] is saying.

There seems to be a great deal of interest for this issue. Could we have just one speaker at a time?

Excuse me. Could we have just one speaker?

Excuse me (pause to gain everyone's attention). *I know all your ideas are important. So, please let's have one speaker at a time.*

Excuse me (pause to gain everyone's attention). *Remember we agreed to have one speaker at a time.* (Point at the ground rules)

These statements acknowledge that a side conversation is occurring without naming the participants or putting them on the spot. For example, you want to avoid hostile statements, such as:

Hostile statements like these will make the situation worse.

Hey! Do you want to share that with the rest of us?

Speak up so everyone can hear you.

If it's so funny, let's all hear it.

Indirect requests almost always win everyone's full cooperation.

Response: Apply structured processes

If side conversations continue after you ask for cooperation, you can adopt structured processes that make it more convenient to cooperate. For example, you could use a speaking prop (see "The Magic Mug," page 59) or a balanced dialogue.

A speaking prop is an object that allows only the holder to speak. Possible props include a gavel, paper cup, or any toy. If the participants are upset over the issue, select a soft object, such as a teddy bear or foam ball. It reduces stress and potential injury if thrown.

Now, you say:

We seem to have great enthusiasm for this issue. So, let's decide that only the person holding the gavel (cup, teddy bear, foam ball) may speak. Is that okay?

Notice this statement begins with a complimentary acknowledgment of the situation (multiple conversations) followed by a suggestion, and ends with a request for cooperation.

A balanced dialogue controls participation by giving each person an equal, measured time to speak. Suggest using this process tool by saying:

It seems everyone wants to talk about this issue. So let's make sure everyone has a chance to be heard by using a balanced dialogue. Is that okay?

I think we need to use a balanced dialogue right now. Is that okay? (a more direct approach)

Use balanced dialogues often.

Situation: Drifting From the Topic

New ideas are wonderful. You want to encourage them, cultivate them, and capture them. You hope your meetings produce countless new ideas during the Idea Harvests. And you write all of them on chart paper, knowing the group will sort the diamonds from the pebbles later.

It's a challenge, however, when new ideas appear during other parts of a meeting. They can destroy productivity by yanking the group's focus from topic to topic without letting them complete anything.

Response: Question relationship to topic

When new ideas seem inappropriate, say:

That's an interesting point (or question). And I wonder how it relates to our topic?

Excuse me. We started talking about our budget and now we seem to be discussing payroll administration. Is this what we want to work on?

We seem to be working on a new issue. I'm sure this is important, and I wonder what you want to work on with the time we have left?

These statements greet the ideas with compliments and requests for clarification. This recognizes that the other person could believe the idea relates to the topic, which it may.

Response: Place in the Idea Bin

You can also use an Idea Bin to manage unrelated ideas. This powerful tool is simply a blank chart page posted on the wall with the title, Idea Bin. Some groups call it an Issue Bin or Parking Lot. The scribe writes new ideas on this chart or the participants write their ideas on Post-it™ Notes that they place on the page.

Direct new ideas to the Idea Bin by saying:

That seems unrelated to our topic. May I put it in the Idea Bin?

That's a great idea. Could you put it in the Idea Bin?

Then, at the end of the meeting, check the Idea Bin. You will find that many of the ideas were resolved during the meeting. Any remaining ideas that have merit can be placed on future agendas.

An Idea Bin proves valuable because it saves ideas while maintaining focus on the current issue.

Valuable Tip
Keep a private Idea Bin. When an unrelated idea appears (active minds have many of them), jot it down and save it until an appropriate time. That frees your thoughts to focus on the meeting.

Situation: Quiet Participants
There are many reasons why someone would be quiet. The person could:

▶ Favor a less aggressive behavior style

▶ Lack interest, knowledge, or commitment

▶ Assume others are more qualified to contribute

▶ Disagree with the approach being developed

▶ Dislike other participants

▶ Feel sick.

Nevertheless, each person in a meeting is a potentially valuable resource. (That's why we invited them.) So, you want to maximize everyone's contributions in the meeting.

Left alone, hidden dissension eats holes in the best of plans.

In addition, when participants hide behind disagreements, they limit their participation. This leads to false agreements, which waste everyone's time. Thus, you must uncover any hidden dissension so the group can resolve it.

Response: Encourage participation

When you notice a quiet participant, ask for contributions by looking at the person and saying:

How do you feel about that, Chris?

What results do you expect from this, Pat?

Chris, How will this affect you?

Pat, How do you imagine this will work?

What do you think others will say about this?

What concerns do you have?

How do you think we should proceed?

Sometimes a quiet participant will test the environment with a tentative reply or a minor, safe point. Respond positively and with encouragement to any response that you receive. Then probe further to explore for more ideas.

Sometimes you can encourage quiet participants to contribute by making direct eye contact, pausing, and letting your face say, *What do you think?*

Response: Use a structured process

A balanced dialogue provides both quiet and dominant participants equal chances to speak.

Tip #1

Most people will respond when asked to talk about their feelings.

Tip #2

Different people have different views on what is too much. A quiet person may feel overbearing after making two statements in an hour. A dominant participant may feel left out after contributing only 90% of the ideas.

Situation: Dominant Participants

Dominant participants contribute significantly to the success of a meeting. They offer ideas, discover solutions, and make decisions. They can motivate others to take action.

They can also overwhelm, intimidate, and exclude others. They can rush people into adopting poor ideas. They can leave others feeling left out.

Thus, you want to control their energy without losing their support. Here are responses that help balance the contributions in a meeting.

The easiest way to get what you want is to ask for it.

Help dominant participants make your meeting a success.

Response: Ask others to contribute

Asking quiet participants to contribute indirectly moderates the more dominant participants. You could say:

Before we continue, I want to hear from the rest of the group.

This is great. And I wonder what else we could do. [Look at the quiet participants when you say this.]

Who else has a thought on this?

Response: Use structured processes

A balanced dialogue equalizes contributions from all participants and the nominal group technique distributes contributions through round robin participation. You can also use a round robin to collect ideas in any of the process tools.

Response: Include them in the process

If you can't beat 'em, join 'em. Or, in this case, ask them to join you.

Some people want applause and recognition. So, you can trade private recognition for public applause by saying:

I need your help with something. It's clear to me that you know a great deal about this issue and have many good ideas. I also want to hear what other people in the meeting have to say. So, I wonder if you could hold back a little, to let others contribute.

I can tell you're an expert in this area. And I wonder if you could help me reach other members in the group. I want them to ask questions and have a chance to discover ideas, just like you've been doing. So, I wonder if you could let them talk first.

Some people may want to lead your meeting. They think leading a meeting is fun (and it is). So, they attempt to take over by contributing tons of ideas on everything, including on how to run the meeting.

If a participant tries to take over, you can retain control by giving away minor tasks. For example, such participants make excellent scribes. They can also distribute materials, run errands, deliver messages, post chart papers, run demonstration units, operate projectors, change overhead transparencies, act as greeters, and in general perform any logistical task related to the meeting.

This approach puts dominant participants in a controlled, prominent role while moderating their attempts to take over the meeting.

Response: Create barriers

Here, simply move away from them and make less eye contact. If you are unable to see them, you are unable to recognize them as the next speaker.

Note that this approach could offend the dominant participant. Avoiding eye contact can imply disapproval, and sending such a message can change a potentially powerful ally into an adversary.

Thus, use this approach with moderation and support it with complimentary requests for assistance such as described above.

Refocus the other person's energy so you both succeed.

Build only barriers that you can easily remove.

Use caution with this one.

Response: Preempt comments

This is an aggressive technique that you can use once, perhaps twice, in a meeting. After that it adopts the subtly of a mace. It works best with people who have a sense of humor and a solid ego.

Just before the dominant participant begins to speak, acknowledge that the person probably has a valuable contribution and then quickly direct attention to someone else. This gives credit with one hand and takes away control with the other.

For example, you could say:

I'm sure [name of dominant participant] knows the answer, and I want to hear from someone else first. (look at others in the meeting)

I'm sure [name] has already figured this out, and I wonder who else has an idea on what to do next.

[name], you're probably way ahead of us on this, and I want to start over here first. (Point toward less active participants)

Notice that each of these statements starts by recognizing the dominant person as knowledgeable, quick, or visionary. Be sure to speak with a pleasant, respectful voice. This will leave the dominant participant feeling complimented and willing to allow someone else to speak.

Valuable Tip

Quiet participants often hope to be ignored; dominant participants want to be noticed. You will be most successful moderating dominant participants by building bridges between what they want and what you need.

Situation: Deadlocked discussions

It happens easily. The process is heading smoothly toward resolution when someone raises a concern. Other participants join the concern. Suddenly a gap appears in the agreement. Some want more data. Others want to continue. Now, the meeting is dead-locked.

Rather than fall into a quagmire of arguments, you could apply the following:

Response: Form a subcommittee

Ask for volunteers from the opposing viewpoints to form a subcommittee to resolve the issue. This is a useful approach, because:

▶ The issue may require extensive research, which is best done outside the meeting.

▶ The people who caused the puzzle will be responsible for solving it.

▶ The effort to resolve the issue will test its priority. That is, if no one wants to spend time finding a solution, then perhaps the issue (or at least the controversy) is unimportant.

Ask for a subcommittee by saying:

There seem to be concerns about this issue. Rather than use everyone's time in the meeting, I want a subcommittee to resolve this and report back to us. Who wants to be on it?

Response: Ask for an analysis

If only a few people obstruct resolution, ask them to analyze the issue and propose alternatives. You can say:

You seem to view this issue differently. Rather than use everyone's time to discuss this further, could you help us understand your position by preparing an analysis of the issue with workable alternatives?

As with a subcommittee, this approach will either uncover essential considerations or test commitment. In either case it moves the deadlock out of the meeting so you can proceed.

If people agree to analyze the issue, treat this task like an action item. That is, define specifically what they will do, who will do it, when they plan to complete the task, and the resources (time) they plan to use. This is important because critics are often perfectionists who can take forever to complete a task. Thus, you want everyone's agreement on the amount of time they plan to spend on the analysis.

Some people are more tuned to finding flaws than others. This is valuable if it leads to improvements, and it becomes a nuisance if it leads to chronic nitpicking.

An important reminder

These tactics apply only when the process in your meeting is deadlocked. Remember that meetings are an excellent medium for resolving differences, exploring disagreement, and achieving consensus. The

Important point

different views of the participants drive creativity to find solutions.

Situation: Filibuster

Sometimes, someone in a meeting will spin off on what seems like an endless monologue. You sit there waiting for the person's battery to run down. But on and on and on the person talks. You have two options: send out for food or intervene.

If you choose to intervene, there are two ways you can respond.

Response: Excuse me.

Use the words *Excuse me* as a wedge to interrupt. It is important that you say, *excuse me* with polite sincerity. For example, you could say:

Excuse me, I feel lost here. I wonder if you could summarize your key point.

Excuse me, this seems interesting and I wonder where it's going.

Excuse me, (face the group) is this what we want to talk about?

Excuse me, I'm sure this is very important and since we have only ten minutes left I wonder if you could please tell us your main point.

I realize *excuse me* can be a sardonic expression. Your tone of voice defines the difference between intervention and disdain. For example, if you say, *Excuuuuuse Meee,* prepare for a counterattack. This approach works when you politely, sincerely, and simply say, *excuse me.*

Response: Overlay words

If you feel more aggressive, you can steal control from the speaker. In this case, cut in to the monologue by repeating the person's last word or words and then rapidly continue with your idea. Although any words will do, this works best if you repeat the end of the speaker's sentence.

This is a verbal hit and run. Start by repeating the other person's words with slightly more emphasis than they were spoken and then continue with your idea in a pleasant voice.

Caution. This requires finesse to make it work.

Important point

It is critically important that you speak with a light, playful sense of humor. You want to appear likable and almost innocent while you perform this dastardly antisocial act.

This sounds like a run-on sentence, such as:

Huge fish-right-and we're talking about ways to increase sales. Pat, do you have an idea on this?

Note that the words *fish, Right,* and *and* are run together as if they were a single word.

Pretzels-good-and we're working on our budget. What else can we do to cut costs?

Sloshed-wow-and we're selecting a new unit for the Western region.

Tip #1
Take a deep breath before you break in. Holding it for a moment will build the energy you need to race through your statement.

Tip #2
This technique is most successful when the other person is talking about something unrelated to the business in the meeting.

Tip #3
Look at the rest of the group while speaking.

Tip #4
Use this with extreme moderation. Overdone, you will appear rude.

Encouragement
Good luck.

Situation: Personal Attacks

Personal attacks are cruel and destructive. They hurt people, mar communication, and end creativity. If they become part of a meeting's culture, they drive the participants into safe and perhaps useless contributions.

In addition, those who attack others steal control of the meeting. I once attended a meeting where one of the participants vented insults, obscenities, and sarcastic comments throughout the meeting. As a result, everyone sat quietly, letting this performer run the show and ruin the meeting.

Attackers appear like giants.

I realize you may feel reluctant to confront an attacker. They often appear larger than life. They spread a toxic cloud of tension that intimidates others from confronting them. So the best way to deal with attackers is to approach their behavior indirectly. You can:

Response: Speak to the Group
Set the stage for the group to enforce its culture by making a general comment. Look at the middle of the group and say:

We agreed to respect each other. (Point to the ground rules.)

This is creating a hostile environment that hurts our meeting.

Just a moment. Let's pause here to calm down. I can tell we're upset about this. And we want to find a fair solution for everyone. (Take deep breaths and relax to model calming down.)

After making these statements pause a moment to let the group respond. Often, someone else will support your request. Then continue as if everything were normal.

Important Tip
Avoid looking at the attacker when speaking to the group. Making eye contact acknowledges and returns power to the attacker.

Response: Explore the Cause
Sometimes people throw insults from behind a fence of presumed safety. They expect to avoid accountabil-

ity. You can disrupt this fantasy by speaking to the attacker. For example, you can say:

Pat, you seem upset with that.

Chris, you seem to disagree.

You seem to have reservations about this.

I realize these statements may sound naive compared to what actually happened. An understated response, however, sounds less threatening, feels easier to deliver, and preserves the other person's self esteem. Realize the attacker may have viewed the attack less seriously than it sounded.

After you speak, continue to look at the attacker and wait for the person to talk about what caused the attack.

If the attacker continues attacking, interrupt with:

Excuse me. We need to respect each other. And I wonder what makes you feel upset over this.

Excuse me. We heard that. Now, what makes you feel that way?

Excuse me. We agreed to respect each other. And I wonder what your concerns are.

Be sure to speak pleasantly or else you could start an argument.

Response: Call a break
If verbal approaches fail to end the attacks, then call a break or end the meeting. This will give you a chance to coach the attacker, rewrite the agenda, rebuild communication, and (if appropriate) schedule another meeting without the attacker.

Response: Coach During a Break

If appropriate, you can coach the attacker. Remember: attempt coaching only when there is a realistic chance of a positive outcome (see pages 119–123 for details).

If you decide to coach someone regarding a personal attack, you can say (in private):

When you told Pat to 'Jump off a bridge,' I felt disappointed because that hurts the teamwork we need to finish this. I want you to express your disagreement diplomatically. Okay?

Situation: Outbursts

An outburst occurs when someone snaps a mental rubber band. What follows is a volcanic eruption of words, anger, and fear.

The most remarkable aspect of an outburst is that the person who blew up may feel more surprised that it happened than anyone else in the meeting.

Response: Interrupt

Thus, you must deal with this carefully and quickly. In a breath, you need to stop the behavior, acknowledge the person's feelings, and call a break (or end the meeting).

When an outburst occurs, say:

Stop! I can tell you're upset. So, let's take a break to calm down.

There are three parts to this statement and each is essential. The word *Stop!* catches attention, like a splash of cold water. The sentence *I can tell you're upset,* shows you understand the person's emotional message. And the last sentence *So, let's take a break to calm down,* leads everyone to a better place.

I realize that saying these words with the right emphasis may be a challenge.

First, hold out your hand and shout, *Stop!* as if the word itself would stop a charging bull. Then speak the next sentence with reducing intensity, so you sound calm by the end. And finally, speak the last sentence with a soothing voice to model the emotional level that you want.

Graphically, it looks like this.

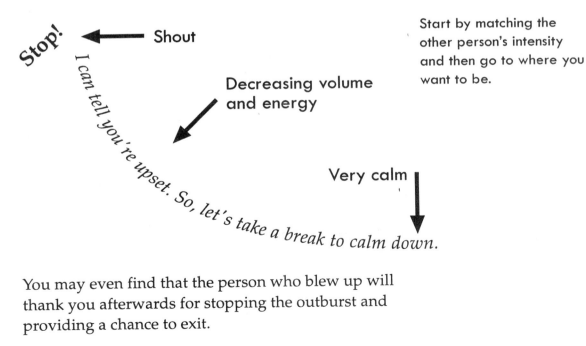

Stop!

Shout

I can tell you're upset. So, let's take a break to calm down.

Decreasing volume and energy

Very calm

Start by matching the other person's intensity and then go to where you want to be.

You may even find that the person who blew up will thank you afterwards for stopping the outburst and providing a chance to exit.

Whether you call a break or adjourn will depend upon the situation. If you call a break, you can resume work on the issue. This has the merit of showing that the outburst only delayed (instead of destroyed) progress.

On the other hand, if you adjourn, you give the participants more time to recover and repair communication. Actually, since adjourning only means taking a long break, in most cases it will be better to adjourn.

A special consideration

People with chronically low flash points may benefit from professional counseling. They may have learned to use outbursts to get their way or they may have emotional challenges raging inside them. Improving their behavior is beyond the scope of this book and anything you would want to attempt. However, if appropriate, you could suggest that the person seek assistance. (Caution: suggest this only if such matters are your responsibility and if you feel confident the other person will be receptive.)

Tip #1

Detach your feelings from the outburst. Avoid showing anger or attempting to overpower the other person. Most people instinctively respond to anger with more anger. That may have been useful in the days of cave dwelling, but in a meeting it can produce a fight. If you interrupt, do so with strength, intensity, and deliberate calm.

Important point

Tip #2
Some of the participants may have been especially disturbed by the outburst. If appropriate you may want to meet with them to hear their concerns and assure them that work will continue on the issue.

▼▼▼▼▼▼▼

Key Ideas

▶ End multiple conversations by asking for cooperation. For example, say: *I'm having difficulty hearing our speaker. Could we have just one speaker at a time?*

▶ Bring a group back to focus by placing unrelated ideas in an Idea Bin or by testing if the idea applies. For example, ask: *How does this relate to our topic?*

▶ Encourage quiet people by asking for their contributions or by using process tools that equalize participation.

▶ Discourage dominant people by directing your attention elsewhere. Also, ask them to let others contribute or involve them in the logistics of the meeting.

▶ Free deadlocked discussions by asking the major proponents to resolve the issue outside of the meeting. Invite critics to prepare an analysis with alternatives.

▶ Interrupt a filibuster gently with *Excuse me*. Then return to the issue.

▶ Counter personal attacks by asking the group for support or by uncovering the cause.

▶ Interrupt an outburst by saying: *Stop! I can tell you're upset. And I think we should take a break to calm down.* Start forcefully and end with a calm, soothing voice.

Chapter 23

Effective Meetings

Yes You Can!

A Final Thought

You can hold effective meetings with any group. The keys are:

▶ Focus everyone's thinking on producing **results** by using structured process tools

▶ Honor the participants by stating positive **affirma**-tions and expectations

▶ Maintain a safe environment by modeling and requesting cooperative participation

Best of success as you use these techniques to hold Effective Meetings.

In an hour or less!

Resources

Glossary

Affinity Diagram
Structured process where the participants write ideas on notes, post notes on a surface, and group ideas by topic. Use this to define concepts and organize complex issues.

Ain't It Awful
Game played where the proponent achieves superiority by denigrating an issue. Claims are usually supported with complex data, case histories, hearsay, and exaggerated conjecture. Bonus points awarded if claims result in a new committee.

Amazing Ideas
Ideas with questionable worth. These may be misunderstood insights, useless distractions, or deliberate attacks.

Androcles and the Lion
Fable (dramatized in a play by George Bernard Shaw) about a man who removes a thorn from a lion's paw and is later spared by the same grateful lion.

Balanced Dialogue
Structured process where everyone speaks for an equal, set time. Use this to gather views on an issue or to collect information.

Ben Franklin Analysis
Decision process where the reasons for and against a decision are listed and compared.

Brainstorm
Structured process for a freewheeling collection of ideas. Use it to find innovations.

Capture the Gold

Game played where the proponent attempts to grab as much wealth as possible before the meeting ends. Wealth can include any resource, such as money, people, commitments, equipment, and materials. A bonus is awarded if the proponent ends up with all the wealth that existed at the start of the meeting.

Cause and Effect Diagram

Structured process to analyze an effect by identifying causes, generally related to equipment, materials, people, and procedures. Use this to analyze an issue for improvements.

Conversation

Freeform dialogue with no agenda. Neither party knows in advance where it will go or how it will end. Often entertaining and purely social, this form of communication aims at building rapport.

Deadlocked Discussions

Activity where the participants are unable to continue toward results on an issue.

Discussion

Unstructured process where a group talks about an issue. Participants attempt to maneuver toward results through wandering focus, misunderstandings, and hidden agendas. Use this (with caution) to gather general ideas.

Dominant Participants

People who contribute significantly more than others in the meeting. Though often an asset, they become a liability if they prevent others from contributing.

Filibuster

Disruptive behavior by someone who delivers an endless monologue.

Force Field Analysis

Structured process to collect ideas on driving and opposing forces. Use this to analyze issues with two or more sides.

Gotcha
Game played where the proponent surprises other members in the meeting with embarrassing information. Winner shouts *Gotcha!* when scoring a hit. Double points are earned when the information relates to an area of prime responsibility.

Ground Rules
Operating principles that define the culture in a meeting.

Hidden Agenda
Privately held expectations and goals that everyone brings to a meeting.

Idea Bin
Place to store ideas that seem unrelated to the issue being discussed.

Idea Harvest
The part of a meeting when participants contribute ideas.

Information Exchange
Type of meeting where a group gathers to trade news. Members participate in proportion to how much they have to say or want to say. Topics are often unpredictable, since they are the news. Attendance can range from few to many. Examples: Staff meetings, shift break meetings.

It's My Mountain
Game played where the proponent builds and then defends a logical fortress. Proponent wins by repelling all pleas to cooperate, compromise, or view an issue differently.

Lectures
Type of meeting where one person speaks to an audience. Audience participation, if any, is limited to asking questions. The size of the audience can range from one to thousands depending upon interest in the topic, reputation of the speaker, or competing events, such as the weather. Examples: Classes, seminars, keynote presentations.

Look at Me
Game played where the proponent engages in activities designed to attract attention. Activities can include boasts of personal accomplishments, clever stories, jokes, satire, sarcasm, and unanswerable questions. Bonus points are awarded when these are combined with humor.

Lose/Lose
Outcome where everyone suffers a loss.

Meeting
A team activity where select people perform work that requires group effort.

Multiple Conversations
Disruptive behavior that occurs when two or more people talk at the same time. (Ideally, only one person speaks while everyone else listens.) Also, called side bar conversations.

Nominal Group Technique
Structured process where the participants collect ideas in a formal round robin followed by discussion and voting. Use this to determine the best option.

Outburst
Disruptive behavior by someone who explodes with anger, fear, and words.

Parliamentary Procedure
Formal guidelines for meetings as described in Robert's Rules of Order.

Personal Attacks
Disruptive behavior consisting of insults, name calling, sarcasm, threats, or other offensive statements.

Plus/Delta
Structured process where the participants collect ideas on *What they liked* and on *What they would like to have done differently*.

Process Tools
Structured activities designed to gather ideas, control discussions, reach consensus, make decisions, or obtain results.

Quiet Participants
People who contribute significantly less than others in a meeting. They represent a potentially valuable and untapped resource.

Robert's Rules of Order
The official guide for Parliamentary Procedure.

Round Robin
Activity where the participants take consecutive turns participating.

Scribe
The person responsible for recording ideas in a meeting.

Shared Achievement
Type of meeting where select people gather to perform work that requires group effort. Ideally, four to eight people attend. When more attend, the process can bog down; with fewer attendees it becomes a conversation instead of a meeting. Example: Most effective business meetings, which is the subject of this book.

Social Meetings
Type of meeting where diverse people gather to further an activity. They may also network, relax, and have fun (often the true reasons for the meeting). Most service, social, or professional organizations hold this type of meeting. The agenda often follows a structure specified by the parent organization. The size of the audience depends upon how many people show up and may range from few to many. Examples: Service organization meetings, Chamber of Commerce mixers, professional meetings.

Training

Type of meeting where people meet to learn skills. The person conducting the training often prepares the agenda. Topics can vary from leadership skills (such as how to conduct effective meetings) to mechanical skills (such as how to operate a drill press). Attendance ranges in size from few to many. This can depend upon how many people wanted to improve or were sent by their boss. Examples: Workshops conducted by consultants or trainers, mass-market seminars.

Trick Questions

Destructive questions because they have no correct answer or they imply the other person suffers from some deficiency.

Unrelated Ideas

Ideas that lack a clear connection with the issue being discussed. These may be creative insights or misleading detours.

Win/Lose

Outcome where one of the parties suffers a loss.

Win/Win

Outcome where all parties gain what they need, or at least where no party suffers a loss.

Suggested Reading

Mastering Meetings
The 3M Meeting Management Team with Jeannine Drew

People Skills
Robert Bolton

Communicate With Confidence!
Dianna Booher

Effective Meetings, The Complete Guide
Clyde W. Burleson

First Things First
Stephen Covey

The 7 Habits of Highly Effective People
Stephen Covey

How to Make Meetings Work
Michael Doyle

How to Run a Successful Meeting in Half the Time
Milo O. Frank

Listening Your Way to Management Success
Allan Glatthorn and Herbert Adams

Guide to Quality Control
Kaoru Ishikawa

Influencing With Integrity
Genie Laborde

Smart Questions
Dorothy Leeds

Thinkertoys
Michael Michalko

Straight Talk
Sherod Miller, Daniel Wackman, Elam Nunnally, and Carol Saline

We've Got to Start Meeting Like This:
A Guide to Successful Business Meetings Management
Roger K. Mosvick and Robert B. Nelson

The Lost Art of Listening
Michael P. Nichols

A Kick in the Seat of the Pants
Roger von Oech

A Whack on the Side of the Head
Roger von Oech

Robert's Rules of Order
Henry M. Robert

Effective Listening
Lyman Steil

The Coach
Steven J. Stowell and Matt M. Starcevich

What a Great Idea
Charles "Chic" Thompson

Power Talking: 50 Ways to Say What You Mean and Get What You Want
George Walther

Index